Minnehaha Creek
Living Waters

by

Jane King Hallberg

EXPANDED EDITION

CITYSCAPES PUBLISHING COMPANY
Minneapolis

CITYSCAPES PUBLISHING COMPANY
James D. Thueson, Publisher
Box 14474 / Minneapolis MN 55414
Tel. & Fax: 612-221-9883

IN MEMORY OF
Captain Earl Christian King
Loving father, inspiring teacher

Acknowledgments

First, I wish to thank the publisher for encouraging me to greatly expand my first Minnehaha Creek book and for asking the questions that led to the discovery of more rare, pertinent material in old books—memories filed in creek lovers' minds—old letters on microfilm—and in archives—and even an heirloom book, *Indian Moons*, unobtrusively tucked away in a relative's bookcase. This book, by Joseph Brown's great-granddaughter, is so rare that it is not in any local historical society's collection. I am glad there was still time to gather Minnehaha Creek material before some of the primary source papers of the 1800s yellow and flake away.

Thanks to my sister, Nan Passolt, for inspiration, creek lore and photos.

Thanks to the Brooklyn Historical Society for the aid and encouragement of its Board of Directors, of which the author is a member, and, especially, to Board Member Leone Howe who helped push the first edition of *Minnehaha Creek - Living Waters* into print.

Thanks to John Baule, former Director of the Hennepin County Historical Society, who gave the first version of this book an encouraging and helpful critique.

Thanks to the librarians and curators of the collections of the Minnesota Historical Society, Hennepin History Museum, Western Hennepin County Pioneer Association, Minnetonka Historical Society, Edina Historical Society, Minneapolis Park and Recreation Board, St. Paul Pioneer Press, Star Tribune, for assistance in my research, particularly for access to previously unpublished material, and for permission to reproduce the photographs credited to them. Thanks to the many families and individuals, including Sharon Siegrist, Wyllys McElroy, Claudia Schuman, Leland Wyman, Roger Bueghy, Margaret Bevan, Avery Stubbs, and Katie Edmunds for allowing me to see and use family letters, diaries, and photographs. Uncredited photographs are from my personal collection.

Cover photo: Minnehaha Falls on July 27, 1990.

Jane King Hallberg

Contents

I ~ The Discovery

II ~ A Canoe Voyage Through History

III ~ Minnehaha Falls and Vicinity

IV ~ Minnehaha Today

V ~ Chronology and Bibliography

Illustrations

I
THE DISCOVERY

Two boys, Will Snelling and Joe Brown, with some soldiers,
explore Minnehaha Creek and discover Lake Minnetonka.
What happened to them after their great discovery?

Brown and Snelling,
Minnehaha Creek Explorers

Two seventeen-year-old boys explored Minnehaha Creek in May, 1822. They canoed a couple of miles upstream on the Mississippi River from Fort Snelling and paddled into the deep, wooded glen of the creek. They could hear the rumble of the falls that was one-half mile upstream. This falls became known as Minnehaha in later years, but it was called Little Falls at the time to distinguish it from the lower, but much wider, St. Anthony Falls a few miles up the Mississippi.

LITTLE FALLS

The boys' plans would take them off the military reservation, which was acquired by the U. S. Government under the contract that Lt. Zebulon Pike made with the Dakotas in 1805. The agreement included ceding approximately nine miles of land on each side of the Mississippi from the Minnesota River to St. Anthony Falls. This left more than half of the most western part of Minnehaha Creek in the Dakotas' region. The creek explorers had no official permission for their trip, which might have brought them into conflict with the native Americans.

Accompanied by two soldiers from Fort Snelling (at that time called Fort St. Anthony), Joseph Renshaw Brown and William Joseph Snelling traveled the twenty-two miles up Minnehaha Creek, towards the west. They would have had to portage around Minnehaha Falls and a drop, or falls, that was at today's Penn Avenue South and also portage around several rapids if Little Falls Creek was flowing fast. After a good part of two days spent paddling upstream, the four reached the source of the creek - the lake that became known as Minnetonka. Although many local Indian people had resolved to keep their Minnetonka paradise a secret, the two boys, Joe Brown and Jo Snelling, had heard from their Indian friends about a large lake a day's journey from Fort Snelling toward the setting sun. A rumor from voyageurs was that the body of water was as large as Lake Champlain.

When the four adventurers reached Lake Minnetonka, they paddled onto it and camped on one of its islands, which today is called Big Island.

COLONEL
JOSIAH SNELLING
*Courtesy Hennepin
History Museum*

JO SNELLING

The four were gone overnight. Among people at the fort, there was evidently concern about the missing explorers because they had gone into a wilderness called the Big Woods where there were lots of bears and where wolves often skulked near travelers by day and serenaded them with eerie howls at night. As mentioned, much of the land they explored was off the military reservation and, in fact, remained so until the treaty of Traverse des Sioux, 1851.

At the time of the trip, 1822, the Fort St. Anthony area was still under construction on a bluff at the confluence of the Mississippi and Minnesota Rivers. The fort was on the northwestern frontier of the United States. Some buildings were ready for habitation the fall of 1822, but it would be two years before all the troops could be housed there. The first buildings were of wood and, later, nearby limestone was used for construction. It was 1824 when the name of the fort was changed from "St. Anthony" to "Snelling" in honor of the new commandant.

The idea for the trip came when young drummer boy, Joe Brown, was looking for a change from the routine of fort and military life. He talked his friend, Jo Snelling, into a voyage of discovery into Indian country. One source says they were looking for places to establish trading posts. No posts resulted, but the boys did gain fame by being the first newcomers to report the discovery of Lake Minnetonka.

The young men who initiated the creek expedition were not greenhorns. Red-haired William Joseph, or Wm. Josiah, Snelling had attended a private boarding school near Boston and then spent two years as a cadet at West Point until age sixteen, when he and the son of Major Hamilton, of Fort Snelling, were discharged from the academy for some infraction of the rules. After that Joseph traveled to the fort in the future Minnesota where his father, Colonel Snelling, was the commander. Joseph's red hair was a bit darker than the colonel's bright, red hair. Colonel Snelling "was greatly attached to him and would do anything for him," wrote fort resident Mrs. Ann Adams, a contemporary of the two Snellings. Mrs. Adams added that "Jo," as he was usually called, "led rather an ungoverned life for some years."

With the relaxed parental reins that his stepmother and doting father used, Jo was able to spend the 1820-21 winter living with the Dakotas in their tepees. Thus, he gained fluency in the Indian language and became a translator. In May, 1821 Jo brought Yankton Chief Wahnatah to the fort to visit Colonel Snelling. This chief, from Lac Qui Parle, was a great chief of the Dakota nation.

Stories about Joseph Renshaw Brown picture him as dashing, smart and inventive in spite of not having much formal education. He was always good natured, even after reverses, and he had a persuasive tone to his voice. Joseph was born January 5, 1805 in Harford County, Maryland. His mother died when he was a baby, and his father, a Methodist Episcopal preacher, moved his family to Lancaster, Pennsylvania to a farm. When Joseph was age fourteen, his father apprenticed him to a printer whom the youth considered harsh and unjust; so Joseph ran away, enlisted in the army and came west to help Col. Henry Leavenworth's troops establish the fort that became Fort Snelling. Starting as a drummer boy, Joseph was a first sergeant when he was discharged from the army in 1825. Later, he attained the rank of major during his re-enlistment at the time of the local war of 1862. JOE BROWN

There was concern at the fort when the boys and soldiers did not show up as expected; so, Colonel Snelling ordered out a search party. Some of the detachment searched up Minnehaha Creek and eventually found the explorers, who were enjoying wild strawberries and fish. In contrast to the two days spent exploring upstream, the trip downstream, back to the fort settlement, took only one day.

The colonel and his family were not happy about this caper, so the matter was quieted down. One punishment the daredevils could have received was a bare-skin flogging, which was used at the fort at the time and sometimes administered by the colonel, himself. Another, more drastic, punishment was exile by being drummed out of the service and put in a canoe without paddles. Then the unfortunate offender was pushed into the river current below the fort to fend for himself in the vast stretch of water and wilderness between Fort Snelling and Prairie du Chien. This actually happened to a young soldier and his wife who had issued bogus money at the fort. However, there is apparently no record of any punishment that the creek explorers received. PUNISHMENT
AT THE FORT

Word got out about the discovery, and several history books mention the Brown and Snelling trip up Minnehaha to Lake Minnetonka in 1822. Because the U.S. government did not allow settlement on territory not covered by treaty, many years went by before settlers could dream about claiming land on the western stretches of the creek. Finally, the land was opened up by the 1851 treaties of Traverse des Sioux. However, enterprising Joe Brown made a claim in 1826 at the mouth of Minnehaha Creek, on the north side, on land that was part of the 1805 Pike land treaty and built a claim cabin there. This was the "first claim in Minnesota," and the creek for many years was known as Joe Brown's Creek according to the *Pioneer Press* of July 25, 1915. This naming of the creek is confirmed in an 1874 atlas BROWN'S CLAIM which contains memorials about Joseph Brown by his friends. Bayard Shaver, a Minnetonka pioneer, also wrote that Brown's Creek and Falls were named for Joseph Brown because of his claim at the mouth of the creek.

BROWN'S FALLS

Minnehaha may have been named Brown's Creek for Joe Brown because of his claim at its mouth and his 1822 explorations there. However, Major Taliaferro, an Indian agent at Fort Snelling, wrote in a July 11, 1856 letter that Minnehaha *Falls* (but not the creek) was named in honor of Major General Jacob Brown, a commander of the U.S. Army, 1814-28. Under orders of President James Monroe and Secretary of War Calhoun, General Jacob Brown gave the command to the Leavenworth expedition to proceed up the Mississippi and build a fort. Whoever the pioneers remembered when they called Minnehaha Falls and Creek "Brown's Falls and Creek," evidence shows that the popular belief of locals, over the years, was that the creek and its falls were named for Joseph Brown.

The two soldiers who accompanied Brown and Snelling on their creek explorations received little notice other than having their names recorded as "Mr. Stewart" and "Samuel Watkins."

Biographical sketches of Joseph Renshaw Brown and William Joseph Snelling show that they were both extraordinary men.

WILLIAM JOSEPH SNELLING

William Joseph Snelling apparently left Minnesota about the same time his parents left, in 1827. While here, he married a pretty—but uneducated—French girl from Prairie du Chien, a union Snelling's parents opposed.

MARRIAGE

"They lived in a sort of hovel for a while, and owing to cold and privation during the ensuing winter, the poor girl took sick and died," remembered Mrs. Ann Adams, a fort resident. Jo came back to Fort Snelling, and then left for Lake Traverse, where he traded with the Indians. In 1826 Jo defended his father's and his own honor, when Colonel Snelling was challenged to a duel by a soldier. The duel took place at an area by

DUEL

Minnehaha Falls which served fort soldiers as a dueling grounds. Jo Snelling was wounded and lost part of the first finger on his left hand. After the duel, his soldier opponent had to face the usual court-martial for dueling.

The summer of 1823, in July, Major Stephen H. Long came to the fort with the purpose of taking a government expedition to explore along the

MAJOR LONG

Minnesota River and to the Red River Valley. Jo Snelling volunteered to go along as an interpreter and assistant guide. Long accepted his offer. During the journey Snelling and other guides told Long about the discovery of a large lake several miles northwest of Fort Snelling, but the lake, Minnetonka, does not appear on the map that resulted from Long's trip. On the expedition, Jo had a violent argument with Long, and he quit the expedition and returned to the fort. This impudent act, justified or not, plus his unauthorized duel and marriage and his expulsion from West Point, so embarrassed his family that they gave little public attention to Jo's positive activities.

Jo married again sometime after his family's return to Boston in 1827. Impetuous and somewhat wayward as a youth, Snelling used his adventures to further a writing career as an adult. He wrote a poem about the Dakotas, "Thunder Bird," which appears in Edward D. Neill's 1878 *History of Minnesota*. Jo also wrote *Tales of the Northwest* and is credited with the story, *Running the Gauntlet*. John Marsh, a Harvard man who tutored young people at the fort in 1823, thought Jo Snelling was close to being a genius. Still literary, Snelling was editor of the *Boston Herald* at the time of his death in 1848.

JOSEPH RENSHAW BROWN

Bright like his friend Jo Snelling, Joseph Renshaw Brown was the star pupil of the Fort Snelling Sunday school class in his teen years. After he left the army at about age twenty, Joe held onto his claim land and cabin at the mouth of Minnehaha Creek but abandoned it in 1830. Brown had started a trading business with the American Indians after he left the army, and by 1831 he had a trading post at St. Croix Falls, Wisconsin and worked for the American Fur Company. Brown was a licensed trader, but his post was a few miles above the point where the boundary line between the Dakotas and Chippewas crossed the St. Croix River. The attraction of the post could lead to possible hostile confrontations between the rival Chippewa and Dakota groups, according to a complaint made to government agents by Chief Petit Corbeau (Little Crow).

Probably because of such complaints, Joe Brown had decided to abandon his St. Croix Falls trading post and left with his fellow traders in late July, intending to resettle near the mouth of the river. Brown and several Frenchmen and their American Indian families were traveling *down* the St. Croix on July 27, 1832 when they met explorer Henry Rowe Schoolcraft and his party as they paddled *up* the St. Croix, returning from their Itasca expedition. They were heading for home via Lake Superior.

As an Indian agent working under the authority of the U.S. Office of Indian Affairs, Henry Schoolcraft stopped Brown's party and examined Brown's trading license, which was satisfactory. He also searched for whiskey in the four, small birchbark canoes of the Brown party, but he found no strong drink; nevertheless, Schoolcraft revoked Brown's trading license for the remaining, unexpired time on it and "permitted him to proceed out of the (St. Croix) country." As a further discipline, when Schoolcraft arrived at the site of St. Croix Falls, he burned the two log buildings at Brown's abandoned trading post, which Schoolcraft called illegal trading houses.

Meanwhile, Joe Brown's party reached the mouth of the St. Croix River and went a short distance up the Mississippi to Oliver's Grove (Hastings), where Brown built a single story log cabin on, according to his later platting, Lot 1, Block 12 of the original Hastings, on the southwest corner of Vermillion and Hastings Streets. Situated in a grove of bur and white oaks, the house was the first built in Hastings, where, it is claimed, he also became the first successful wheat grower in Minnesota.

After a Chippewa treaty negotiation in 1837, Joe Brown returned briefly to the site of Taylors Falls on the St. Croix, where he engaged in trading and lumbering.

In about 1835, Joseph Brown met his future wife, Suzanne Frenier, when she was seriously wounded by a gunshot. Daughter of Dakota-Scotch Abigal Crawford and a French fur trader, Suzanne (or Susan) and her family lived among the Dakotas near the post that Brown ran for the American Fur Company on Lake Traverse. Suzanne was the young daughter of Narcisse Frenier, who was in charge of the nearby post of the Columbia Fur Company.

SCHOOLCRAFT

HASTINGS

JOSEPH
RENSHAW
BROWN
1805-1870
SUZANNE
FRENIER
BROWN
1819-1904
*Courtesy Hennepin
History Museum*

According to writings of Suzanne's great-granddaughter, "Beautiful was Suzanne as the white dawn, petite, with a waist so small the two hands of great-grandfather could span it." (Winona Blanche Allanson in *Indian Moons*) In the forest one day, Suzanne inadvertently walked into the line of fire at the target range used by men from Joseph Brown's trading post. She was seriously wounded, and rescuers carried her to Brown's post. He sent a runner to Lac Qui Parle to get the Reverend-Doctor Williamson, the missionary there. With the combined skills of Doctor Williamson and healing herbs and roots supplied by Indian medicine men, Suzanne recovered. This incident led to a romance between Brown and Suzanne, and they were married not long after they met.

GENEALOGY OF JOSEPH R. BROWN'S WIFE, SUZANNE (OR SUSAN),
AND HIS GREAT-GRANDDAUGHTER, WINONA BLANCHE ALLANSON
AS GLEANED FROM ALLANSON'S 1927 BOOK, *INDIAN MOONS*

Waanatan, of the dynasty of Red Thunder,
head chief of the Confederated Sioux nation
[or, "Five Lodges" forty miles west of Lac Qui Parle]
and his wife
|
Their daughter, Wenonah, married
Colonel Crawford, a Scotchman in the British Army
|
Their daughter Abigal Crawford (Muzadawin)
[sometimes erroneously referred to as Winona Crawford]
married
Narcisse Frenier, French fur trader
|
Their daughter, Suzanne Frenier
(her Indian name meant "Soft Down") married
Joseph Renshaw Brown
|
Their daughter, Ellen, married
Lt. John S. Allanson, 20th U.S. Infantry
|
Their son, Henry Gray Allanson, married
Alice Mertie
|
Their daughter, Winona Blanche Allanson,
was Joseph Brown's great-granddaughter.

SUZANNE'S
GENEALOGY

NAMING
MINNESOTA

Brown's destiny was to become prominent in the shaping of Minnesota — even to its name, which came from the Dakota language that he knew so well. The name "Minnesota" is derived from the Dakota word "minisota," meaning slightly milky, "sky-tinted water." Long ago, in explaining it, an Indian woman pointed to a place in the Minnesota River that had this characteristic.

Joe Brown was skilled in the Dakota language because his wife was of Dakota-Scotch-French lineage and also because he used the Dakota language as an Indian agent and trader. Called the Hon. Joseph Renshaw Brown, he served in the Wisconsin Legislature for St. Croix County, most of which was in the future Minnesota, in 1840-42. There he suggested the name "Minnesota" for the new territory that he envisioned. "He urged the organization of Minnesota Territory and advised the present spelling of Minnesota," according to Volume X, *South Dakota Historical Collections*, page 382. The naming and spelling of Minnesota by Joseph Brown is confirmed in *The St. Paul Pioneer Press*, July 25, 1915.

MINNESOTA TERRITORY

Hon. Henry Sibley and Hon. Morgan L. Martin proposed this name for the new territory, in 1846-48, to the United States Congress, and Minnesota Territory was voted into existence on March 3, 1849.

Over the years, Brown lived at Mendota and St. Croix, among other places, including trading posts he had at Land's End on the Minnesota River, about a mile above Fort Snelling, in 1831; a post at Chan Wakan, on the west side of Grey Cloud Island, sixteen miles below St. Paul; and a post at Big Stone Lake at the time of his death.

PIG'S EYE

It was Joe Brown, the first justice of the peace in the Territory of Minnesota, who contributed his humor to the fact that St. Paul was called Pig's Eye in its early days. Brown was at his trading post on Grey Cloud Island where he had virtually unlimited jurisdiction as justice of the peace. A tough old voyageur named Pig's Eye and a young man both claimed the same quarter section of land at the site of St. Paul. They agreed to ask Brown to settle the matter. Brown knew he had no authority over land titles, but he saw a chance for a joke and told them to strip for a sixteen-mile race to the contested claim, where the winner would post a notice and have title to the land. The young man started running fast, but the wily old Pig's Eye paced himself at a sensible speed and put up the first notice. Subsequently, the area became known as Pig's Eye until renamed "St. Paul."

Some Brown firsts:

BROWN FIRSTS

Drummed the first reveille at Fort Snelling
Explored Minnehaha Creek and discovered Lake Minnetonka
Laid out the first townsite in Minnesota - part of Stillwater,
     which he called Dahkotah (His claim there was about 1839)
Built the first Territorial public road, from Fort Snelling to
     Prairie du Chien—drove the first team over it
First to cut and raft lumber down the St. Croix
Helped organize the state agricultural society
First general of the state militia
Laid out Brown's Valley and Henderson

In 1852-54 Brown was editor and publisher of *The Minnesota Pioneer*.

Despite his lack of formal schooling, editor Brown could "dash off . . . twenty sheets of foolscap in a single night" that were accurate and technical, according to one of his friends in a memorial speech. Another good friend, Gen. James H. Baker, said of Brown:

> He was the Warwick of his day, and outwitted politicians called him "Joe the Juggler."

As an Indian agent in Minnesota under President Buchanan, Brown had the duty of getting supplies from steamboats in St. Paul to the western Minnesota border reservations. The only means of transport at the time was on the backs of voyageurs, or by dog sleds or Red River carts pulled by oxen, at speeds of only ten or fifteen miles a day. While he was at Henderson in 1859, Brown developed the first self-propelled oxless-horseless carriage vehicle in Minnesota. In the summer of 1860, Brown fired up his three-wheeled steam wagon, or traction motor, and created a sensation on the Fourth of July by towing people in an attached wagon through Henderson. The back wheels of the steam wagon were twelve feet in diameter, with a tread twenty inches wide, to help push it over the roadless prairies. The front guiding wheel was about three feet high. Fuel was wood.

That autumn, with Beers Johnstone, Brown's relative, in charge, Brown took the rig on a trial run of forty miles to Fort Ridgely. Near the fort, the

AGENT BROWN WITH DAKOTA CHIEFS, 1858, WASHINGTON, DC

Standing: Brown, A.J. Campbell, Chief Has-a-War-Club, A. Robertson, Chief Red Owl, T.A. Robertson, N.R. Brown [Joseph's brother] Sitting: Chief Mankato, Chief Wabasha, H. Belland

The Dakota were of the M'dewakanton or Wapekute Band, Lower Sioux Agency.

Courtesy Hennepin History Museum

steam wagon became stuck, hub deep, in the mud and drifting snow, and they had to abandon it. It remained on the prairie during the Civil and local warfare, and the smokestack was riddled by bullets. When peace came, Brown hauled the vehicle's boiler back to Henderson for use in a gristmill.

Brown was enroute to New York to oversee the manufacture of another steam wagon when he heard about the outbreak of war between some of the Dakotas and the government in 1862. His family and new home were on the Minnesota River in the midst of the trouble. He was also very concerned because as Indian agent at the Upper Sioux Agency, circa 1860, he had successfully taught and settled over one hundred Indian families on farms. Then, in 1861, he was removed as Indian agent under the spoils system. Some of the Dakotas did not like the new appointees at the agency, and this is cited as one of the contributing rubs that made a spark turn into the conflagration of the 1862 bloody local war. Brown turned back at Chicago on his way to New York and hurried to Minnesota, where he enlisted with the rank of major and hoped to learn the fate of his family.

BROWN'S STEAM WAGON
Number Two
1862
Courtesy St. Paul Pioneer Press

MANSION

At the time of the outbreak of trouble, the Brown family was living in western Minnesota in their new granite-stone, nineteen-room mansion that Brown had a builder put up on a walkout site on the north bank of the Minnesota River in 1861. Called a castle sometimes, the house was sixty feet in length and thirty feet wide. Located about ten miles above today's Redwood Falls and seven miles down the river from the Upper Sioux Agency, the house was a mecca to travelers and prospective settlers in the frontier wilderness.

Big and imposing, the house had elegant furniture from New York and a billiard room adjoining Brown's study on the top half story. There was a full-width porch overlooking the river on the two middle levels. In customary frontier style, guests were always welcome and were entertained with food, lodging, hunting, fishing, horseback riding or just visiting, all without charge. Brown's large family liked a good time.

One sunny day when the birds were singing and all seemed right with the world, Brown's son Samuel and daughter Ellen were home from their respective boarding schools, Shattuck College and a school at Georgetown, D.C. (now a part of Washington). Just a few months before, Ellen had attended President Lincoln's inaugural ball.

The two set out on an errand to deliver the family wash to an Indian laundress at Hazlewood, the mission of Doctor Williamson and Reverend Riggs. Driving a horse-drawn vehicle on what was later called the Sibley Trail, they passed by Little Dog's village, and he warned them to tell their mother and family to flee to a place of safety as there was fighting at the Lower Agency. No one else they met knew of any trouble except an old Indian woman who whispered that there was danger and they must warn their mother. Unbelieving at first, the family fled early the next morning after another warning from a French-Canadian neighbor. Their old clock struck four as they grabbed a few possessions and left home in the dark, with neighbors that included two Ingalls girls, in three wagons pulled by oxen. After six miles of travel over the prairie, they were surrounded by Dakota warriors who were hiding in the tall grass. Mrs. Brown stood up in her wagon, waving her shawl, and shouted out in Dakota the names of all her distinguished Indian relatives and that she expected protection for herself and the whole party. Captured August 19, 1862, the group was taken to Little Crow, who gave them protection, but it was an uneasy period and they had six long weeks of captivity. In conversations with Little Crow, who was related to Suzanne Brown through her half-brother (Gabriel Renville), Mrs. Brown sensed that he was sad that events had forced the warfare.

Meanwhile, unable to reach his family, Brown was on active duty with the army. In one action Major Joseph Brown joined about one hundred fifty soldiers and civilians in a march to bury the dead near the Lower Agency. The party was surprised in an attack by the Dakotas at Birch Coulee. Many were killed or wounded, including Major Brown, who was seriously wounded. This battle was in early September, and it ended when reinforcements came on orders of Gen. Henry Sibley. Ironically, Brown had to fight against some of the people he knew well and whose cause he had championed for years in treaties and in adapting to new ways. When General Sibley's troops reached Camp Release, Brown was with them, and he was reunited with his wife and family, who had stayed safely at the house of Little Crow and in the tent of A ke pa, Mrs. Brown's stepfather. Unfortunately, their beautiful, new mansion on the Minnesota had been set afire during the warfare, destroying wood parts and furniture—although the granite and plastered walls survived the scorching well enough to give evidence of the skillful construction methods used on the house. Some of the foundation is still evident in 1990.

By 1863, Brown was again with the troops of Sibley at Roberts County.

SIOUX UPRISING

SUZANNE BROWN'S HEROISM

BATTLE OF BIRCH COULEE

DESTRUCTION OF THE MANSION

He was chief of scouts at Stony Lake (Crystal Springs, North Dakota) in June, 1863, and he estimated the opposition forces there as four thousand to five thousand warriors. Later Brown helped locate and build Fort Wadsworth (Fort Sisseton) for the government and became the fort's military agent. That duty finished, he moved his family, about 1865, to Brown's Valley.

On a trip to New York, Brown felt well, but he died in his sleep, presumably of a heart attack, in a New York hotel on November 9, 1870. He had gone to New York, with a friend, to supervise construction of his latest steam wagon. In his papers, survivors found he had designs for a touring car almost identical to cars manufactured some years later.

MONUMENT Joseph Renshaw Brown was buried in the cemetery which he had planned and started years before, on a hilltop, at Henderson, Minnesota, overlooking one of the waterways he canoed, the Minnesota River. Around 1910, townspeople installed a tall, granite monument, encircled at the top with lights, in Brown's memory, and this landmark could be seen for miles around the countryside at night. A current map shows a Joseph R. Brown State Wayside on the Minnesota River about ten miles above Redwood Falls. This is the site of the Brown Mansion ruins. Some official archaeological digs have uncovered Brown family eating utensils, china, flat irons and remnants of furnishings such as Mrs. Brown's grand piano. The house site is marked with a plaque at the Wayside, which is eight miles south of Sacred Heart on Renville County Road Number 9. The spot is on the Minnesota Historical Society's list of forty-five major historical sites in their publication, *Minnesota's Major Historic Sites*.

That's the summary of what happened to the boys after they explored Minnehaha Creek and discovered Lake Minnetonka!

II
A CANOE VOYAGE THROUGH HISTORY

The Headwaters of the Creek
An Overview
The Mills and Yesteryear Along the Creek

Detail from Davison Map: TWENTY-FIVE MILES AROUND MINNEAPOLIS, 1881
Corrected to 1884 by Geo. W. Cooley, Civil Engineer
The six mills are marked with stars. Going downstream: Minnetonka Mills, St. Albans,
Minnehaha (Schussler's), Waterville (Edina), Richfield, and the original Minnehaha Mill.
Map courtesy Wyllys McElroy.

Chapter 2

The Headwaters of the Creek at Lake Minnetonka

Exactly one hundred years after the exploration of the creek by Brown and Snelling, this author's folks built a house about a block from the creek on Fifty-third and York Avenue South; and, over the years, our whole family became creek aficionados. As adults, the four offspring of our family knew the creek had a very beneficial effect on the quality of our lives. We pondered about what went on in the creek environs before, during and after our childhood on the creek. This resulted in a history voyage down the creek, which included samplings over many years as we traveled along Minnehaha Creek by canoe at various times—once substituting a slow, two-person rubber raft for a short trip.

CREEK SOURCE
GRAY'S BAY
LAKE MINNETONKA

For example, on a sunny August day in 1984, after a substantial rainfall, my sister and I went to Minnehaha Creek's headwaters at Grays Bay, Lake

Minnetonka. Water was pouring through Grays Bay dam, built in 1979 between the lake and the creek. This dam replaced dams constructed at this spot in 1897, 1932 and 1944.

Two young boys were standing in about three feet of water by a walkway in front of the dam, and the forceful lake waters were giving them a whirlpool bath. In the air was the faint, sweet smell of fresh Minnesota sky-blue water as it began a journey that could blend it with salt water at the Gulf of Mexico.

On one of our checkup visits to the dam, in 1988, we saw that a little fishing dock, which was about twenty feet below the dam, was gone; but a boat-launching site was still on the lake nearby. No water was coming through this time. Today's dam consists of three concrete bays, each one about ten-feet wide, with metal gates. Cable controls on the gates can be used to regulate the amount of water going from Minnetonka under the sluice gates into Minnehaha Creek.

The ordinary high water mark for Lake Minnetonka, established by a Department of Natural Resources survey, is 929.4 feet above sea level. The lake has reached this but normally is about a foot below it. The Operating Plan for Grays Bay dam is under the authority of the Department of Natural Resources, taking into consideration a number of factors such as time of year, creek flow and lake level. The D.N.R. works with the Board of Managers of the Minnehaha Creek Watershed District and issues a permit to the latter. The creek is the only surface outlet of Lake Minnetonka, although there may be unknown ground water discharge.

DISCHARGE RATE

Basically, the Operating Plan for the creek allows the watershed district to discharge water into the creek if the lake is 928.6 feet above sea level. By the permit in effect in April, 1987, the Department of Natural Resources authorized the Minnehaha Creek Watershed District to allow 90 gallons of lake water per second through the dam into the creek at the level mentioned. At the time of the permit, April, 1987, Minnetonka's level was 928.25 feet above sea level after the driest winter since 1853. Then in July, 1987 there was the "two hundred year" rainstorm which flooded the creek and made the falls near its mouth a roaring cascade.

Lake Minnetonka is a very large lake, the largest in Hennepin County. It is really a series of connected lakes. A glacial, morainic lake, formed in hollow places in the glacial drift, Lake Minnetonka follows the pattern of such lakes, having irregular, winding shorelines, bordered often by hills.

Beaches and shorelines at this lake are usually sandy, and Minnehaha Creek, its outlet, is also sandy in most places. Minnetonka was at times called Peninsula Lake for obvious reasons.

Apropos of the magnitude of the lake, its size is described below:

Twenty-five bays
Shoreline: Approximately 125 miles, including islands
Surface: About 14,043 acres
Average depth: Thirty feet
Area of the lake: Twenty-two square miles

Creek admirers always hope for a high water level at Lake Minnetonka because it is Minnehaha Creek's water source. Various surprising ways to keep Lake Minnetonka water levels up have been suggested over the years. One suggestion was to divert Crow River flood water in an eleven-mile ditch to the lake. Another idea was to put in pipelines from the Mississippi or Minnesota Rivers to Lake Minnetonka.

Starting in 1938, a water pumping solution worked. Seven pumps and wells were installed at Minnetonka at a cost of $270,000. They pumped artesian water continually for two years and in that time raised LakeMinnetonka's level forty-nine inches. The summer of 1942, from rain and pumping, the water went over the dam at Grays Bay into the creek, and the pumps were turned off. Up to March, 1965, the pumps had not been used except for tests, dry spells or lake aeration; and today the pumps are either gone or not operational.

Currently, in early 1990, some Lake Minnetonka residents are urging that the pumping of ground water be resumed to bring the lake up to what they consider a desirable level. However, the opponents of pumping suggest that advocates of pumping would have a difficult time convincing authorities that such action would pose no environmental threat—or even that the lake level should be managed instead of leaving the matter to Nature.

A CREEK OVERVIEW

Minnehaha Creek threads like a a vein of silver from Lake Minnetonka through west and southwest suburbs of the City of Minneapolis and on through the south edges of Minneapolis until the creek drops in a waterfall which measures about fifty-three feet. The beautiful waterfall called Minnehaha Falls, near the creek's mouth on the Mississippi, first received widespread attention when poet Henry Wadsworth Longfellow romanticized it in his *Song of Hiawatha* poem-book, published in 1855. Visitors to Minneapolis, from tramps to presidents and princes, *had to* see the falls because of the poem.

Also in 1855, another poem about the creek and falls was published. The poem, "Minnehaha," by a local woman, a schoolteacher, Frances A. Shaw, appeared in a book called *The Genius of the West*. Here is an excerpt from her two-page poem:

At my feet a smiling streamlet danced in careless glee along,
And with that solemn anthem, blent its lightly gushing song.
And I traced its silvery windings till its sparkling waters fell,
Bounding, leaping, gaily dancing o'er the rocks, adown a dell,
Where a scene of wondrous beauty was unfolded to my eyes,
That enthralled my raptured spirit in a wild and glad surprise . . .
And this was Minnehaha, these were then the "laughing waters,"
That echoed once the laughter of the forest's dark-eyed daughters.
Here, from summer's heat retreating, would the Indian hunter stray,
And bare his fevered forehead to their cool light-falling spray. . .

Minnehaha Creek and Falls evidently furnished inspiration for the following polkas and songs:

Minnehaha or Laughing-Water Polka by Francis H. Brown, N.Y. (1856)
Minnehaha Polka by Mrs. S. L. Lara
Indian Lament by Antonin Dvorak (1893)
While We Dream of Minnehaha's Love by Rosso and Erickson
Minnehaha Slumber Song by Griffith and Shardlow (1903)

MILLS

The practical, business possibilities of the creek were what others saw in the fast water and rapids, and millers envisioned mill wheels turned by the creek's waterpower. Several entrepreneurs' dreams came true. Six sawmills or gristmills, or both, were built and operating at six locations on Minnehaha Creek during the last half of the 1800s.

ZOO

Robert F. *Fish* Jones, who had a zoo on the site of the present Basilica of St. Mary, saw the creek as a perfect backdrop and new location for his zoo, which no longer fit in very well in the downtown district of Minneapolis, He bought property and started his Longfellow Gardens Zoo on the banks of the creek near Minnehaha Falls in 1906, and soon the creek's banks played host to seals, lions, tigers, camels, elephants, bears, birds and other animals.

As far as recreational use, various former creek residents mentioned old swimmin' holes at Minnetonka Mills, by the Terwilleger house on the island near today's St. Albans Mill Road; at Schussler's Mill in St. Louis Park, at Xerxes Avenue and, nearby, at York Avenue at a former bend in the creek. On Pleasant Avenue, around 1917, there used to be a popular swimmin' hole at the remnants of a dam, and still another swimming place was on Portland where there was a diving board, circa 1917.

Other sports made possible by the creek and its valley were hiking, sliding, skiing, skating and fishing. ·

With this overview of the creek's history in mind, we started our history voyage down Minnehaha's living waters—*living* because of the creek's invigorating treasures such as water, food, pleasure, peace, beauty,

MINNEHAHA POLKA

sparkles, sound, wildlife, vegetation, recreation and waterpower.

Chapter 3

Minnetonka Mills

The beginning of Minnehaha Creek could have looked much the same as today to the young men who discovered the creek's source in 1822. As one looks straight down the creek from the dam's walkway, there are no visible buildings. Today there is a pond of open water that leads into Minnehaha as it passes through a wide area of marsh grass on both sides. About twenty-two miles of the meandering stream lie ahead.

The first two and one-half miles for a canoeist on the creek includes passing under the Highway 494 bridge. Near the Burwell House, Minnetonka Mills, some rapids appear, and they give a sample of how a mill wheel was turned by the fast water here in the last half of the 1800s. From the East McGinty Road bridge, near the Burwell House, our view in August, 1984 was of two boys floating through the rapids on inner tubes and on down the creek out of sight. Pushed by the fast current caused by recent rain and water flowing through the dam at Grays Bay into Minnehaha Creek, the boys clutched their tubes as they sped past the stores and some of the houses that make up the Minnetonka Mills settlement.

As we looked west from the bridge, heavy foliage almost hid the historic house called the Burwell House. The scene could have been back a century. This Victorian-style house belonged to a prominent mill manager and owner, Charles Burwell. The house has been restored to its 1880s look.

The view in the other directions was of buildings of Minetonka Mills, which started with a dam and mill at this site years ago in the 1850s. A rippling in the long grass on the high creek bank drew our attention to a woodchuck which was waddling towards the water—a reminder of the wilderness that was once here.

HEZEKIAH HOTCHKISS

Another wilderness scene pictures the storied pioneer Hezekiah Hotchkiss, in the summer of 1852, canoeing on what he called *My Lake,* referring to the lake later named "Minnetonka." Echoing from the woods beyond the lake where it flows into Minnehaha Creek, Hotchkiss heard the sound of someone chopping down trees. The ring of the axe was, in effect, a toll announcing a new era at the lake and creek. Hotchkiss knew intuitively that the paradise where he lived, canoed, trapped and fished—

much like his Indian friends—would be changed forever by the new settlement. Originally from Boston, he lived in a log cabin on a high point right by the lake. He had an Indian friend who was both a protector and companion, and he did not often get lonesome for his friends and relatives in Boston. Incidentally, Hotchkiss must have thought of himself as Robinson Crusoe of the lake wilderness area because he referred to his faithful Indian companion as "Friday."

Hotchkiss claimed he was the only resident paleface around Lake Minnetonka up to 1852, but now there were others. The axe blow reverberations he heard came from the site of Minnetonka Mills where Simon Stevens, Calvin Tuttle and James Shaver were preparing a site for a claim cabin and sawmill. Another day Hotchkiss and his aide were canoeing along the southeast shore of the outlet lake and saw a man driving stakes and "stepping off land," as Hotchkiss put it. This would have been James Shaver, who made a squatter's claim, with lakeshore on the present Grays Bay, shortly after Simon Stevens made his claim at the mill site.

STEVENS AND TUTTLE

The men—whom Hezekiah Hotchkiss regarded as interlopers on his and the Dakotas' stamping ground—officially "discovered" their mill site near the beginning of Minnehaha Creek and Lake Minnetonka in April, 1852. Simon Stevens made a claim there, and Calvin Tuttle bought an interest in the mill in 1854.

Young and single, Simon Stevens provided inspiration for the trip to see if they could discover the "big water" of rumor; and Calvin Tuttle, a millwright, provided the know-how of maturity. The two probably became acquainted at the home of Simon Stevens' brother, Col. John H. Stevens, the first of the new settlers to build a house at the site of today's downtown Minneapolis, on the west side of the river. Calvin Tuttle, who built the second house on the west river bank, was a neighbor. Tuttle's log cabin was down the river from Stevens' house, at what would be about Seventh Avenue South and a little east of the site of the old Milwaukee Depot.

Note: Two sources record a little-known trip which Simon Stevens and Calvin Tuttle made to the site of Minnetonka Mills in 1851. Eli Pettijohn wrote that the trip was made in October, 1851, shortly after he told Simon Stevens' brother, John, that "Minnehaha Creek was the outlet of the lake and that by following the creek he would find the lake." Pettijohn had been there.

Louise Burwell also gave 1851 as the date of a preliminary scouting trip by Stevens and Tuttle up Minnehaha to its source before their much-publicized 1852 discovery of the extent of the big lake (Minnetonka). The men were looking for water power potential on the creek, and they came to a beautiful cascade where they considered building their sawmill, no doubt at the former falls at Penn Avenue. However, their Indian friends urged them on up Minnehaha Creek to the site of Minnetonka Mills where they decided to build a sawmill and city.

Miss Burwell, a long-time resident near the Minnetonka mill and a graduate of the University of Minnesota, recorded a very believable and detailed story of this almost-forgotten creek trip that Stevens and Tuttle made in 1851, which was also the year that they applied to the Territorial Legislature for permission to build a twelve-foot dam at their proposed mill site.

For more about Louise Burwell's creek story, see Chapter 7 herein. Pettijohn's article appeared in *The Minneapolis Journal* for January 3, 1903.

THE RE-DISCOVERY

On their so-called 1852 discovery trip to their Minnetonka sawmill site, Simon Stevens and Calvin Tuttle packed a week's provisions and their guns and blankets and started out from what is now downtown Minneapolis on April 8, 1852. They hired a team to take them as far as the road went, to a point on Minnehaha Creek about nine miles from its mouth. They hiked along the north creek bank until they reached the outlet lake (Grays Bay on Lake Minnetonka), and they crossed the ice to Big Island where they camped. The ice was still about three-feet thick that April. The next morning, they explored the big lake further and discussed the possibility of steamboats on the lake. Then they came back along the western shore and camped on the south side of the outlet lake.

The third day, Stevens and Tuttle left the outlet bay and came down the creek to a point about "fifty rods above the site of the present (as of 1895) dam in the village of Minnetonka" where the current and solid banks were very suitable for a mill dam, as recorded by Atwater in his *History of Hennepin County* book. Here Simon Stevens made a squatter's claim; STEVENS CABIN and the two men returned the following week with two more men to start clearing for Stevens' claim cabin. By June of 1852, Simon Stevens' cabin, built of lumber from St. Anthony, was on the site.

Apparently, the first discovery of Lake Minnetonka by Joseph Brown FIRST DISCOVERY and Will Snelling thirty years before was forgotten in the mists of time. FORGOTTEN The Stevens and Tuttle discovery of Minnetonka's vastness and great resources was called the event of the year in *The Minnesotian* newspaper of September 11, 1852.

Note: "So, when it was noised abroad (in 1852) that a new lake, of surprising magnitude, had been found in the vicinity of St. Paul, persons here and there tossed their heads, and said, they knew those who had visited the same spot years ago," wrote Elizabeth Ellet in her book *Summer Rambles in the West* about a trip she took out to Lake Minnetonka.

Joseph Snelling, in 1823, accompanied Major Stephen Long on his explorations along the Minnesota River, and Snelling told Long about the big lake; but neither the creek nor the lake appear on Long's 1823 map of the expedition's route.

American Indians had enjoyed and hunted by "Minne Tonka" for many years; and the French were there at an early date. An old French pistol and remnants of an old French log fort (or two-story house) and word of mouth—all give evidence that some of the early French fur traders were on, or near, the lake in the 1700s.

Nevertheless, two old maps show Lake Minnetonka was practically unknown and unrecognized for its size as late as 1849 because the maps show no lake as the source of Minnehaha Creek. Both the J. N. Nicollet map, from 1836-43 surveys, and the 1849 Map of the territory of Minnesota by Captain John Pope (of the Corps of Topographical Engineers) show a creek, or its falls, marked "cascade," in the vicinity of Fort Snelling; however, wavy lines for the creek trail off to the west and end with no lake source shown. Looking back, it is obvious that the catalyst for the Stevens and Tuttle rediscovery of Lake Minnetonka was the 1851 Traverse des Sioux Treaty which opened the land for settlement.

Elizabeth Ellet on an August, 1852 visit to Stevens' cabin, said it "stood on a wide peninsula formed by a bend in the stream." Just below this, the creek rushed down a beautiful rapids, "giving the value of a fine water-power to the locality." The party had crossed the creek enroute to the site, so it was evidently on the south side of the creek. Dana Frear also wrote that he believed the cabin was on the south side. In her 1853 book, *Summer Rambles in the West,* Mrs. Ellet said Stevens' cabin was "built of rough boards, with pretty wide crevices between." It was small and low, with no shade, with paths through the brush to the creek, and a spring some distance away from the cabin. Through the open door, she could see a bed of straw, with a blanket and mosquito netting, which took up about one-third of the shanty. The other side of the room had a large cook stove and two shelves which held tin pans, platters and larger pans. A tin wash basin, small mirror and towels were the only "toilet conveniences." A small table, wash tub, wooden pails and jug for spring water were other furnishings.

ELIZABETH
ELLET

THE STEVENS AND TUTTLE SAWMILL

The sawmill entrepreneurs were well known in the settlements on both sides of the river at St. Anthony Falls. Groups often gathered in the home of Simon Stevens' brother, John, to make plans for town projects. The other partner, Calvin Tuttle, was the first treasurer of Minnesota Territory. As soon as possible, after the signing of the 1851 Traverse des Sioux Indian Treaty, Stevens and Tuttle and some partners secured permission from the Minnesota Territory legislature to build a twelve-foot dam on Minnehaha Creek at the site of Minnetonka Mills.

SAWMILL

Note: The 1851 Treaties of Traverse des Sioux and Mendota signed over to the United States government (in combination with earlier land cessions) most of what is now the southern half of Minnesota, except two Dakota reservations along the Minnesota River, in exchange for certain payments.

After U.S. ratification, these treaties opened the Minnehaha Creek valley for settlement as well as the Lake Minnetonka area. Regarding the eastern part of the creek on the Fort Snelling military reservation—this reservation was reduced in 1852. Claims could be made but legal titles in Hennepin County did not become available until 1855.

INDIAN TRAIL

A major Indian trail, which ran from the village of the Ojibwas near Mille Lacs Lake, via Anoka, to the Dakota village at Shakopee, crossed the creek at the site of Minnetonka Mills at the time of the dam and mill construction activities. The Dakotas also used the trail in going between the Wayzata and Shakopee areas. There was a lot of travel on the trail.

In late June of 1852, Simon Stevens led a group of prominent Minnesota Territory residents as they poled and rowed two bateaux up Minnehaha Creek to view the large lake that Stevens and Tuttle had rediscovered. Included in the party were Stevens' brother, John Stevens, Territorial Governor Alexander Ramsey, Ramsey County Sheriff George Brott, Judge B. B. Meeker, Dr. Alfred Ames, John C. Cairns, Edgar Folsom, Jack Haney and Simon Garvey.

NAMING LAKE MINNETONKA

From Stevens' cabin, they poled and rowed their boats two and one-half miles upstream in Minnehaha Creek to the creek's source lake. After exploring part of the lake, they came back down the creek to Stevens' cabin for supper and an overnight stay in the new claim cabin. Chatting after their good supper, provided by the hospitable Stevens, Governor Ramsey asked Simon Stevens, "Stevens, what are you going to name your lake?" Stevens replied, "Governor, the lake has already been named by the Indians who call it *Minne* (water) *Tonka* (big)." Governor Ramsey said, "Good, then we'll call it *Minnetonka*. Ever since, it has been known by that name, and, of course, the names for Minnetonka Mills and the suburb of Minnetonka spun off the name of the lake.

In an article a few months after the lake was named, Col. John P. Owens, editor of *The Minnesotian*, published in St. Paul, commented that the lake really should have been named *Mdeatonka*, which meant "big lake" in the Dakota language. Owens felt the latter name was more definite than the "big water" name, *Minnetonka*. However, he said, the Minnetonka "name has already started, and has gone abroad to the whole world, (therefore) the change cannot be made without great inconvenience."

The same year that Governor Ramsey and party visited Simon Stevens' claim shanty via bateaux, another group of men went out there by land, struggling through, in some areas, roadless countryside. Col. John Owens of the weekly, *The Minnesotian*, was with the group and wrote an eyewitness account of this trip in early fall to Lake Minnetonka and Stevens' cabin. The article covered most of two pages in the small newspaper of Saturday, September 11, 1852. A condensation follows:

Without mentioning the Brown and Snelling discovery of Lake Minnetonka in 1822, publisher Owens wrote that it was incredible that such a large body of water as Minnetonka, only fifteen or twenty miles from St. Paul and St. Anthony, "could not have been known by anyone else to exist . . . until this year." Many old Indian traders spoke of a large lake, or series of lakes, in the direction of Minnetonka, "but until the explorations commenced early this spring by Messrs. Tuttle and Stevens, nothing like a correct idea of the topography of this region was entertained."

Nine men left St. Anthony, Minnesota Territory, on Monday, September 6, 1852 with the intent of making a rather hurried exploration of Lake Minnetonka, with Simon Stevens' claim shanty as their base of operations. Those on the trip were:

Col. John P. Owens	A. Murphy
Secretary Wilkin	Mr. Miller (John P. Miller)
Col. John H. Stevens	Mr. Lennon, an Englishman
Dr. Alfred E. Ames	Ed Murphy
Mr. T. Porter	

Secretary Wilkin was Alexander Wilkin, Secretary of Minnesota Territory, 1851-53. The Brisette house mentioned below was the Edmond Brisette house on the east shore of Lake Calhoun, where Brisette lived to hold a claim for Rev. E. G. Gear.

BRISETTE HOUSE

The road the party took went five or six miles across "the most beautiful prairie in America," Owens wrote, until they stopped at the Brisette house on the shores of Lake Calhoun for a few moments' respite for their horses. Then they followed the northern shores of Lake Calhoun to Cedar Lake. The party saw no cedar trees near Cedar Lake. "It is a beauitful little sheet of water, and a great place for fish," Owens commented.

From Cedar Lake, the party's route was almost due west over very rough country. The road west of Lake Calhoun was rough and difficult to go over with teams. There was good soil, with hazel and wild cherry bushes, but very little timber—also, plenty of water for stock, hay meadows and, far to the right, tamarack groves and other timber. After four or five miles of what Owens described as "poundings and joltings," they came, on their left, to another beautiful little lake which they named "Lake Wilkin" after one of their group.

"Three or four miles on, we came for the first time to Little Falls creek (Minnehaha), which we crossed. The land along this creek is good, and mill privileges plenty. The growth of weeds, grass and hazel is as high as a man's shoulders. The surface, however, is too much broken to invite settlement while less elevated and depressed sections remain open. Crossing one of the high peaks hereabouts, while the team was making the circuit of a wet meadow, we found a bunch of the wild sage. . . . We were not before aware that it grew in this country. The whole of Minnesota is a rich and inviting garden for the explorations of the botanist, and we wish greater attention were paid to this matter."

Further on, to their right, the group saw a high peak, from which, according to hearsay, one could see Lake Minnetonka, the Minnesota River, the Mississippi River, the village of St. Anthony and St. Paul. Four miles before reaching Simon Stevens' claim shanty at the site of Minnetonka Mills, the travelers had to "take water" (Owens wrote) and travel along Little Falls Creek. At the end of the four miles, they were in front of Stevens' shanty.

DANA FREAR   Simon Stevens did not live at his claim cabin for any length of time but just made visits out there, according to Dana Frear. Frear wrote that the "high peak" mentioned above may have been on the northwest corner of the intersection of Cedar Lake Road with County Road 73, which was known locally as Pilot Knob.

OWENS: REGARDING STEVENS' SHANTY

"This is situated on the creek, and is the end of land journeying and the port of entry for Minnetonka. It is the claim of Mr. Simon Stevens (brother of J. H.) and as fine a mill privilege as can be found in Minnesota. The creek is about two rods wide, and from two to six feet deep. The water is clear with gravel and rock bottom. Mr. Stevens is now hauling lumber to build a mill. The location selected for this purpose will allow him to raise a head of five or six feet. This spot cannot be far from the geographical centre of the county of Hennepin, and may one day be the county seat. A comfortable and welcome shanty is this of Stevens' with a good, whole-souled fellow, Mr. Shaver, inside of it. He volunteers to become our cook, not only for the present occasion, but for the trip up the lake; and so here we unpack."

Simon Stevens was not there at the time; but his brother, Col. John Stevens, was busy planning a future courthouse and village square site. Two men from St. Anthony, Messrs. Morrison and Frost, had come out by buggy to join the party. The Doctor (Ames) and Mr. Miller went fishing and immediately had luck and caught fish enough to feed all twelve hungry men. Fishing for about twenty minutes more, they brought in more bass—a total of about forty pounds. Owens commented, "It appeared sinful to take more than could be used for supper and breakfast; but just after sundown an incident occurred which kept a large quantity of them from spoiling on our hands." Four men arrived from St. Paul. They were looking for cranberries. The four were hungry and noisy and ate lots of fish. After supper, they pitched their tent beside Stevens' shanty.

Owens said the four "St. Paul boys" entertained the others with dance, song and yells until late in the evening. Sometimes, in a quiet moment, they heard the howl of a wolf in the distance. Then they slept. As there was not room for everyone in the shanty, five men slept outside on buffalo robes. A couple pranksters gently rolled the sleeping English neophyte, Lennon, off his buffalo robe onto the bare ground under the wagon tongue. Lennon kept sleeping, and in the morning there was one very mad Englishman!

At eight in the morning, they went, in two bateaux, up the creek to Minnetonka. They entered the present Grays Bay, which writer Elizabeth Ellet had recently named "Browning," in honor of Elizabeth Barrett Browning. According to Owens, the greater portion of this "eastern arm" was covered with wild rice, rushes and water lilies.

Then the party went on exploring Lake Minnetonka, and Owens gave a detailed description of the lake. At a point named "Morrison" (after the man who had joined them at the cabin), they went ashore and walked through pea vine, nettles and ginseng. There they saw a sugar maple tree which was three feet in diameter—also, there were white oak, white hickory, white ash and basswood trees. They only went halfway up the chain of lakes and had to turn back home the next morning.

Newspaperman Owens mentioned the "whole-souled fellow, Mr. Shaver" at Stevens' cabin; and this would have been Stevens' and Tuttle's friend, James Shaver, who was living on the mill site because he had been hired as head carpenter for the sawmill-building project. Shaver at first stayed at either his own crude claim cabin or at Stevens' larger, more comfortable shanty.

As stated earlier, Shaver's claim was over by the outlet lake. Shortly after he arrived, James Shaver had hiked up Minnehaha Creek a few times to a pebbly beach on Minnetonka. On one of his walks back through the woods, he saw an attractive spot and made his claim there, two miles west of the mill area. This squatter's claim was north of the present Minnetonka Boulevard and east of County Highway 101, including the site where Groveland School was built in later years. An 1860 Hennepin County map shows the claim as that of Shaver and (W. S.) Chowen, who was James Shaver's brother-in-law. Their land included lakeshore on what was then called the Outlet Lake (Grays Bay).

Stevens had lumber from St. Anthony hauled out for the sawmill, but first the mill company carpenters built a rough boardinghouse. (Later, a permanent structure, the Minnetonka Hotel, was built sometime in 1853, and it is still standing in the fall of 1989.) Shaver arranged to live in the boardinghouse and to board the crew of carpenters. He sent a message to his wife, Sarah, and their son, Eldridge, to join him in the west. They were at the time living in the lumber town of White Haven, Pennsylvania.

Upon her arrival, Mrs. Shaver accepted the task of running the new boardinghouse, and she was the sole woman there for the first few months. She boarded the mill carpenters and, sometimes, also served meals and gave lodging to travelers. She served three meals a day to the crew of a dozen hungry men who worked on the mill all winter and through March, 1853. Mrs. Shaver had to be butcher and baker. She butchered and cleaned wild ducks or geese, scaled fish and baked bread every day for just the basic menu. Sometimes potatoes or pie were an extra treat.

Shaver, with the help of the mill crew during the 1852-53 winter, chopped logs for a house on his claim. In spring, Shaver and his crew put up a house which measured 18 by 26 feet, with one and one-half stories. The house had an oak shake roof. As soon as the sawmill was completed in March, the Shaver family moved to their unfinished log cabin. That March and well into the summer, the Shavers used bed quilts for both floors and doors on their house. All summer smudge pots were kept smoldering to keep out mosquitoes because the spaces between the logs had not been chinked—perhaps because of the priority to get the mill running. In this setting on August 12, 1853, Sarah Shaver gave birth to twins, Bayard T. and Bernard G. Shaver.

As a doctor was not available, Mrs. Alfred B. Robinson, from a claim in the present Wayzata area, was summoned to help. (Robinsons Bay at Lake Minnetonka today commemorates the family name.) Exhausted, Sarah Shaver had Mrs. Robinson helping out again when the twins were three weeks old. All were settled down and sleeping on the ground in the cabin when, towards morning, Mrs. Robinson awoke because one of the twins was fussing. She reached over and felt an animal's furry paw coming through a crack in the log wall and "pulling the baby towards the crack," according to recollections of one of the twins years later. Mrs. Robinson went out the blanket-covered door to the side of the cabin, and a startled wolf ran into the woods.

A WOLF IN THE NIGHT

One of the Shaver twins, Bayard T., became a teacher at Groveland School and a farmer in the summer. Later, he was Assistant Superintendent of Hennepin County Schools. His twin, Bernard, became a carpenter and a joiner.

The wide, twelve-foot dirt dam at the mill also served as a bridge to cross the creek where the East McGinty Road bridge is today. The sawmill building, started in October, 1852, was finished in March, 1853. It stood on the south creek bank just below the dam. In May the mill started production, and settlers at Lake Minnetonka got lumber at very reasonable prices. In the woods there was oak, elm, ash, hickory, maple, red cedar and basswood. Local lumbermen claimed Minnetonka oak was equal to any in the world.

THE FURNITURE FACTORY YEARS

The sawmill was destroyed by fire in 1854. Then Calvin Tuttle's brother-in-law, Hezekiah S. Atwood, came to the scene to build a replacement sawmill near the old site on the south creek bank. After the fire, Stevens and Tuttle sold their interest in the company to Messrs. Sears, Eastman and Atwood. By 1855, the new sawmill was in place on the first floor, with a furniture factory and warehouse above it. Hezekiah Atwood was manager of both.

ATWOOD HOUSE

The furniture factory had machinery to make chairs, rockers, beds, chests, stools and dressers on turning lathes run by the water wheel in Minnehaha Creek. Besides the lathes, there were upright and circular saws, planes, boring and sanding machines. A newspaper said machinery was on the way for a flour mill but that did not happen. By 1856 the sawmill and factory had thirty or more employees, and two hundred bedsteads and one thousand chairs were produced each week. Three hun-

dred beds and two thousand chairs weekly were being produced by August the following year, with added employees.

For several weeks in the spring, at spawning time, one man had the duty of watching the flume to try to keep the fish out, but there were so many fish in the creek that they often stopped the mill wheel. About two wagon loads had to be shoveled out and given away one year, an old-timer recalled.

A paint and varnish shop was downstream a short distance from the mill, near the present Bridge Street. Abbie Tuttle Atwood, wife of the furniture factory manager, ran the paint shop for the furniture factory. She varnished chairs, bedsteads, rockers, cradles and kitchen storage chests, using any of fifty stencils to beautify the pieces. The much-used Indian trail, mentioned earlier, which crossed the creek at the site of Minnetonka Mills, passed in front of the paint shop door. Travelers on the trail often stopped to talk with Mrs. Atwood.

At Minnetonka Mills today, Plymouth Road, Bridge Street and Baker Road follow close to, or over, the old Indian trail. This jibes with the notes of a man born in 1893 (E.C. King), who wrote that "the first overland roads in Minnesota were the old Indian trails which followed the lines of least resistance and were always the shortest and most practicable routes from center to center."

The Atwood house at Minnetonka Mills was just east of the present Burwell School on the north side of the creek. The 1854-built house had board siding and a fairly high peaked roof with a chimney at one end.

HEZEKIAH ATWOOD
ABBIE TUTTLE ATWOOD
Courtesy Avery Stubbs

PAINT SHOP

Atwood's daughter, Mrs. Perry Gilmore, nee Emma Atwood, thought it was the first house in Minnetonka Mills. This, of course, would not take into account the Stevens cabin or the two early "hotels." Atwood's family lived in the house until 1857, and the house lasted until about 1900 when it crumbled and was cleared out.

There were several tragedies and setbacks, over a few years, that struck the sawmill-furniture factory. Competition from Minneapolis increased, and there was the financial panic of 1857. That was the year that the factory manager, Hezekiah Atwood, fell into upper Lake Minnetonka while buying logs to float down the lake and creek to the mill. Atwood found it necessary to remain at his work in wet clothing in cold weather, and the pneumonia that followed was the cause of his death in spring, 1857. He was thirty-four years old. The cold water, it turned out, had doused the dreams and ambitions Atwood had when he came west to Minnesota Territory, which he had heard was the land of opportunity. Intrigued by glowing accounts by his brother-in-law, Calvin Tuttle, of the great resources of waterpower and forests for mills and the fertile soil for farming, Atwood brought his wife, mother-in-law and his daughters to Minnesota to seek their fortune. Suddenly, his bereaved wife had to support the family.

MILL
TRAGEDIES

Another tragedy occurred when Nathaniel Butterfield drowned while doing a good deed. Butterfield was the foreman and skilled cabinetmaker at the furniture factory, starting in 1855. His wife worked at the factory, also, caning chair seats. Butterfield drowned October 18, 1859, when a freight sailboat capsized in a sudden squall while he was helping the Morton Stone family move from near Stubbs Bay back to the mill area where Stone also worked. Because they were waiting for the weather to calm down, they started out late in the evening and at Starvation Point (Orono Point) a strong wind caught the sails and flipped the boat on its side. The cast-iron kitchen stove slid in first and then other furniture and goods. The boat was icy, and the Stones, their two children and Bob Loveland and Butterfield were drowned. Only one person on the boat, teenager Bob MacKenzie, was able to hang on until the mast hit bottom and stuck in the sand near what is today called Northome. He was able to swim to shore and bring the bad news to the people at the little milling village.

That fateful night some of the folks back at Minnetonka City were waiting for Butterfield to play his violin at a dance; but the fiddler's body was not found until spring, in the lake near Ferndale. In the local paper, James Shaver, the pioneer who had supervised building the original mill, wrote that Minnetonka City was under a shadow of gloom. Butterfield is an ancestor of some of the Stubbs of Stubbs Bay.

In 1857 the widowed Abbie Atwood became manager of the Minnetonka

Hotel near the mill. Some of the guests her daybook listed were: John Stevens, Bishop Whipple, Nathaniel Butterfield, William Ferguson and Charles Galpin. Mill employees also stayed there. Later, mill proprietors Thomas Perkins and Charles Burwell lived at the hotel. Burwell's daughter, Louise, was born at the hotel.

With three little girls to support, Abbie supplemented her hotel income by custom sewing work. For instance, one of her notations shows that on her birthday, June 14, she was "making two shirts for George Odell for 60¢."

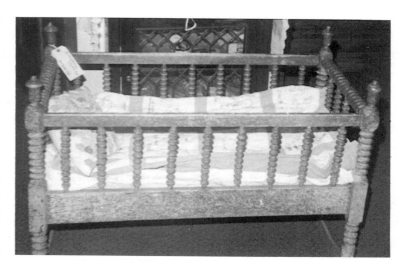

The Atwoods' daughter, Jennie, had a small doll bed which was made at the mill furniture factory. "We dressed up frogs for dolls," she recalled in a 1947 interview when she, Jennie Atwood Pratt, was one hundred years old.

When started, the Minnetonka Hotel was managed by Mr. William Harrington, Simon Stevens' cousin. Wayzata settler, Harry Wakefield, described *Mrs.* Harrington's role when he quoted: "Mrs. Harrington tended to make smooth the rough places of those crying in the wilderness. . . .she took us in and made a shakedown on the floor."

By the time Abigail Atwood took over as manager of the hotel, it was a summer tourist inn. Aristocratic southerners sometimes came out from St. Anthony to the wilds of Minnetonka and stayed at the hotel. Mrs. Atwood left her management job in 1860, but the hotel continued to be a social center of the area, with young people holding dances and parties there in the 1860s.

Abbie Tuttle Atwood left a notebook which contained some of the recipes she used to serve the boarders and stagecoach passengers who came to the Minnetonka Hotel for meals in 1857 and a number of years after that date. Among the recipes: Cream Pie, made from sweet cream, flour, salt, lemon, egg and sugar—Lemon Sponge Cake, which called for a pound of sugar and ten eggs—Fruit Cake, containing raisins, currants, citron and spices— Raisin Cake, which contained a pound of flour and a pound of sugar—a white

CRADLE MADE IN THE MINNETONKA FURNITURE FACTORY 1850s
Courtesy Western Hennepin County Pioneer Association

MINNETONKA HOTEL DEMOLISHED 1991
Drawing by Dave Rodum Minnetonka Historical Society

cake, Ocean Cake—two recipes for Ginger Snaps—and a butter cookie, Bakers Cookies—plus a Coffee Cake which contained one cup of coffee.

Among the other goodies that Mrs. Atwood served at her hotel by the creek were:

LOAF CAKE - 12 lbs. flour, 8 lbs. sugar, 6 lbs. butter, 4 lbs. raisins,
    12 nutmegs, 6 eggs, 1 pint yeast, 1/2 pint brandy,
    1 quart new milk
     "This was Mother's recipe," Mrs. Atwood wrote.
APPLE SNOW - Four tart apples, pared, quartered and steamed-When
    nearly cold add the white of one egg and one cup of white
    sugar and beat one-half hour
RAISIN PIE - One cup chopped raisins, 1/2 cup sugar, 1/2 cup molasses,
    five round crackers rolled fine, 1/2 cup butter, two teaspoons
    cinnamon, one teaspoon cloves, 1/2 of a peppercorn, a little
    salt, 1/2 cup sugar, 5 cups boiling water
A NICE DESSERT PIE - Make a crust as for pie only. Do not roll as thin.
    Line a pie tin. Pare, quarter and core good, tart apples. Lay
    them nicely in the dish. Pour over them a cup of sweetened
    cream with lemon and bake brown.

THE END OF THE FURNITURE FACTORY

1850s CUPBOARD
MINNETONKA
FURNITURE
FACTORY

One hundred people worked at the sawmill-furniture factory at its peak. Minnehaha Creek was essential for the mill which provided a living for them and their families. Pioneer F. J. Butterfield described a balmy day in May, 1858:

"At that time the old factory that had been running for years was going full blast...turning out chairs, rockers, tables and bedsteads. The bedsteads were made with high ends, so mosquito bar could be placed on the bed as there were no screens on the cabins. The wood for the furniture [came] from logs...cut around Lake Minnetonka and floated downstream to the mill. Back and east from the mill were the lumber yards, covering an acre or more of ground [where the blacksmith shop was later and near the paint shop]."

By Mr. F. J. Butterfield, recorded by A. Stubbs in the March 18, 1926 *Hennepin County Enterprise.*

Due to the deaths of the two key employees, furniture factory manager Hezekiah Atwood and cabinetmaker Nathaniel Butterfield, as well

Courtesy Western Hennepin County Pioneer Association

as some serious accounting and financial troubles, the furniture factory was closed down by 1860. The town lost some settlers. The sawmill, however, continued a "meager and uncertain existence" according to

Bayard Shaver. In a disastrous fire on June 8, 1868, the mill was destroyed.

At least two secondary sources say the sawmill fire was in 1860; but added to Shaver's statement above, there are some accounts that point to the sawmill part of the mill burning in 1868. To cite two of them:

"The old Foster saw mill at Minnetonka was burned to the ground on the 8th of June." *The Farmers Union*, a grange paper, Minneapolis, July, 1868.

Edward Bromley, in the *Minneapolis Journal*, December 29, 1902, wrote that the mill lasted about seventeen years after its beginnings in 1852.

THOMAS PERKINS BUILDS A MILL

In 1869 Thomas Hooker Perkins bought six hundred forty acres, which included the old mill site. By fall of that year he had a new three and one-half story flour mill there and also built a cooper shop. As many as thirty-two coopers built barrels there. The cooper shop was near the paint shop on the south bank of the creek just below the bridge on Bridge Street. Each cooper completed his own barrels, and each had a small dock in Minnehaha Creek to which he tied hickory or willow sprouts to soak and soften. Then they could be used as barrel hoops without breaking. They were split in half, and the flat side was nailed to the barrel staves. The sprouts were bought from local farmers who were clearing their land, and a great deal of the stave wood came by steamboat from May's sawmill at Excelsior. Some of the coopers were: Ed Eidam, the head cooper, and Charles D. Burnes, William Houston, Thomas Bryant, Charles Lyons, James Riddle and John Calahan according to a listing in a Dana Frear manuscript. The barrels they made held about 198 pounds of flour, or two sacks.

Thomas Perkins was age fifty-five when he built his mill. His son, Edward, age twenty-seven in the 1870 census, worked in the business with him. Father and son are both listed as "Flour Manufacturer" in the 1870 Federal Census.

Edward Perkins' children were fond of the mill area and were sad when the mill was sold in 1871 to H. M. Vroman and E. H. Hedderly. Part payment was a farm at Excelsior Boulevard and Shady Oak Road, Hopkins. The farm home was later known as the Garfield farm and, still later, as the Hoflin farm, according to Dana Frear in his writings about Minnetonka Mills. Among things the children would miss were the ducks that Grandma Ann Perkins brought to the millpond to eat wastes from the mill. The ducks decorated the pond and became fat and healthy, furnishing meat and eggs for the Perkins family.

> Note: After Edward Perkins left the milling business and decided he did not take to farming, he trained as a doctor and became a prominent doctor in the town of Excelsior, starting in 1878. There Doctor Perkins had a plant to manufacture "Excelsine" antiseptic dressing made out of a mixture of various

clays. Some called the plant his "Mud Factory." Perkins served for many years on Excelsior's board of health. In 1905 the doctor hired four streetcars and took two hundred friends over the new line to Lake Harriet, Minnehaha Falls, Fort Snelling, St. Paul, White Bear and Stillwater.

The flour mill stood on the sawmill site. Dimensions were 32 by 44 feet and three and one-half stories, with three runs of millstones. It was operated by creek water power. In 1874 the mill was sold to the Minnetonka Mill Co., with Loring Fletcher, president, Charles Loring, vice president and treasurer, and C. H. Burwell, secretary.

THE BURWELL YEARS AT THE MILL

Starting in 1874, Charles Burwell was the manager and secretary at the Minnetonka mill at the town then called Minnetonka City. Charley worked for the Minnetonka Mill Company. Eventually, he became the mill owner. An 1876 picture shows the mill with a dormer in the top half-story. Also in this picture are several smaller buildings, two boxcars, two high chimneys, the mill office and the millpond. This is the mill that Thomas Perkins built in 1869.

Burwell had a small steamer, *Fresco*, which ran between the Minnetonka City millpond and Lake Minnetonka. The steamer carried passengers and freight. The *Fresco* was a propeller boat—as distinguished from a steamboat with a stern-wheel or a pair of side wheels (paddle wheels). The propeller was invented in the latter part of the 1830s by Swedish-American engineer John Ericsson and by the English inventor Sir Francis P. Smith. Both men, independently, patented screw propellers; and twin-screw propellers were first used in England about 1860.

BURWELL'S STEAMER
Courtesy Minnetonka Historical Society

The first steamboat on Lake Minnetonka, the *Governor Ramsey*, was a fifty-foot side-wheeler. It carried mail from Excelsior across Lake Minnetonka and down Minnehaha Creek to

Minnetonka Mills. From there the mail was brought to St. Anthony, or Minneapolis, by stagecoach. Several other steamboats, such as the fifty-four-foot *Rambler*, were of light draft also and could reach the mill area by the shallow creek and deliver grain and supplies to the mill.

Under owners, Fletcher and Loring, and manager Burwell, the mill could produce three hundred, and sometimes four hundred, barrels of flour daily. It had a storage capacity for fifty thousand bushels of wheat, with a crew of eighteen men.

Wheat for the mill, over the years, was hauled in by farmers. Some came by barges which were towed over Lake Minnetonka by small steamboats and then down to the mill. However, the larger part of the grain came by rail over the spur track, which was built to the mill by the St. Paul, Minneapolis and Manitoba railroad (renamed the Great Northern later) and also on the Minneapolis and St. Louis railroad tracks.

Charles Burwell, in effect, named Minnetonka Mills. At first the settlement was known as Minnetonka and, later, Minnetonka City. After the Minneapolis and St. Louis Railroad put a station at the mill in 1881, people going by train to Lake Minnetonka on an outing often got off at the mill when the conductor announced "Minnetonka!" Some would find they were still eight to ten miles from the place on the lake where they were headed, and they would go to the mill office and persuade Charles Burwell to hook up his horse and buggy and drive them to their destination. After many such occurrences, Burwell asked the Minneapolis and St. Louis Railroad to add the word "Mills" to the Minnetonka station, and they did, probably about 1882. The name Minnetonka Mills had no official

MINNETONKA MILL
AND MILLPOND, 1876
OFFICE IS AT THE
EXTREME RIGHT
Courtesy
Hennepin History
Museum

NAMING
MINNETONKA
MILLS

origin, according to mill historian Dana Frear.

During the 1874-1884 period, there was usually enough water in the creek to keep the millstones grinding; however, improvements over the years included a one hundred horsepower steam engine to supplement waterpower, making the mill building five stories, and replacing the run of stone with rollers. In that ten-year period, the mill that Burwell managed produced flour that was the equal of that from Minneapolis mills, and the flour was sold in eastern states and Europe as well as locally. The cooper shop there was 24 by 80 feet, two stories, with room for up to thirty coopers making barrels.

The Minnetonka Mill Company sold the mill in 1885 to Messrs. Dawes and McKenzie of Toronto, Canada for $96,000 cash, and "the property changed hands immediately," reported Milton O. Nelson in the *Northwestern Miller* of November 22, 1899; however, no milling took place due to financial entanglements of the owners. Eventually, Charles Burwell bought the mill property back and was going to start the mill, but Hennepin County authorities sought to buy the milldam to solve complaints up and down the creek about water levels. By 1885, owners of fashionable summer resorts and lakeside residents did not want a private corporation to have the power to raise and lower their water line. There were also complaints from Schussler's mill and the Edina mill about water levels. There were threatened and actual lawsuits.

Grasshoppers and chinch bugs had lessened wheat crops over the years, and competition from Minneapolis was critical. Another problem was trying to keep enough water in the millpond to drive the sixty-six-inch American turbine water wheel, which provided free power as opposed to auxiliary power.

Burwell would not sell his dam to Hennepin County; and the court condemned the dam, giving it to the county for $12,000. The County replaced the old dam with one which was one foot lower, but to satisfy continuing complaints, they moved it to Grays Bay. This outlet dam at Grays Bay, built in 1897, robbed Minnetonka Mills of its role as a port on Lake Minnetonka and made it extremely unlikely that any consistent waterpower industry could be revived at the Mills. Charles Burwell wrote on February 19, 1901, to the Department of the Census that the mill never turned a *mill wheel* from 1884 to January 1, 1901.

GRAYS BAY
DAM

With the closing of the mill in 1884, Charlie Burwell took an office job with his former employers and commuted to Minneapolis by train. In 1902 he was the cashier of the Minneapolis post office. The Burwells continued living in their Minnetonka Mills home, and Burwell was a leader in his local community and had served as postmaster of the village from 1877 to 1894.

George Baker of Minnetonka Mills wrote in his diary for April 25, 1895,

"They are taking down the old mill at Minnetonka. It was there before I was born," and he was correct. Some of the machinery had been sold. In 1897, Charles Burwell sold the mill building, including the ground lease, to S. G. Neidhardt, who put new siding on the dismantled flour mill and let advertisers paint it "with flaring advertisements of Minneapolis dry goods and beer," according to the *Weekly Northwestern Miller* of November 22, 1899. Neidhardt tried to turn the mill into a feed mill, by a *steam engine.* The reopening attempt was not very successful as the mill seemed "hoodooed," according to the newspaper mentioned, and "the creek has dwindled to a little run, up which a minnow could hardly work his passage in midsummer," wrote reporter Milton Nelson. Later sources report Neidhardt moved the mill building to southeast Minneapolis in 1901.

After the mill was rebuilt in southeast Minneapolis, cereal foods were milled and manufactured in the old mill until December 25, 1902, when the remodeled structure burned into ashes and scrap iron.

At least two news articles recalled the mill's days at Minnetonka Mills. One, in *The Minneapolis Journal* of December 26, 1902, had the headline of "Historic Structure Gone" and said the mill and warehouse loss was $20,000. The second article, by Edward A. Bromley, recounted the history of the old Minnetonka Mills mill, which burned at Delaware Street and the Milwaukee tracks in southeast Minneapolis, in an area called Little Pittsburgh, that Christmas day, 1902. Bromley's story included the fact that the mill was moved out, leaving Minnetonka Mills without a mill. He wrote:

> When Sam, the falsetto-voiced brakeman on one of the Minneapolis and St. Louis lake trains, rushes into the coaches and yells "Minnetonka Mills," strangers naturally gaze out of the windows expecting to catch a glimpse of the village, but there is no sound of rushing stream, no whir of machinery and no mill. Between the track and a handsome country house, standing on elevated ground at the left, close to the station, a narrow brook winds its way in summertime, dividing the beautiful lawn, which marks the spot where the millpond once reflected surrounding objects, and the miller's sons took their first lessons in the art of swimming. The stream disappears under a wooden bridge at the extreme right, finding its way out through the open sluice of the dam that in the old time used to bar its progress and thereby diminish the flow of water over Minnehaha Falls.
>
> Excerpt above from *The Minneapolis Journal*
> Monday Evening, December 29, 1902

Bromley mentioned the Burwell children, and there were four. Two were from Burwell's first marriage—Anna and George, and two were from his second marriage—Louise and Loring. Untimely death struck two of the children, Anna and Loring. Anna went into ill health after the death of her daughter from burns in an accident, and Loring died from the lingering ill effects of a test-furnace accident that occurred where he worked in New York. Their father, Charles, died in 1917.

Mary Dunham Burwell came to reside at Minnetonka Mills as the bride of Charles Burwell, a widower originally from Connecticut, later of Dane County, Wisconsin. When Mary married the mill manager, she was twenty-one. Their wedding date was October 29, 1876. At first the newlyweds lived in the Minnetonka Hotel, which was built by the Stevens and Tuttle sawmill company in 1853.

THE BURWELL HOUSE

In 1883, during the peak prosperity of the mill under Burwell's management, Charles Burwell built a large, interesting Victorian house on grounds on the north bank of the creek, just west of the mill. The house had a small tower room that overlooked Minnehaha Creek, the mill, lawn, woods and millpond. In summer, boys could often be seen at the mill pond, using it for their swimming hole.

MARY BURWELL Mary Burwell is remembered for working cooperatively with her husband as he served as secretary and manager of the mill. She made bread samples that produced sales. Another example of her remarkable character is the story of her ride of ten miles to get five thousand dollars in gold to pay farmers for their grain. Driving the pacer, "Old Jeff," she hid the gold under her groceries, bravely riding alone on the rural road back to the mill. West of Hopkins, a man jumped out of the bushes just ahead of her, and Mary whipped the reins on the horse, making him gallop away from the possible threat.

Mrs. Burwell also worked for the Christian church. Noticing that a former chapel was used as a school, she stirred up interest in building a new school and pushed until the church was reconsecrated as St. John's Episcopal Chapel. Bishop Whipple preached there several times, and he retained an interest in the little chapel and the Burwell family. The Burwell's daughter, Louise, never married and continued to live at the Burwell house after the death of her mother in 1933. She resided at the house until LOUISE BURWELL 1958 when she sold the property to the William Smith family. Louise was a graduate of Minneapolis North High School and the University of Minnesota, where she majored in languages and mathematics; but she did not want to teach and did not have to work to support herself. She busied herself with community work such as the DAR, Victory Aid work during World War II and the Red Cross. Like her mother before her, she helped

start a church. Louise and George Burwell donated land, and after a ten-year campaign, she saw St. David's Episcopal Church built across the creek, near her home. Church groups often met in her living room. After she sold her home, Louise lived in a little millhand cottage on the grounds for a while; then she moved to California where she died in 1967. The Burwell house, now a museum of several rooms, was purchased by the City of Minnetonka in 1970. Built in Italianate style at a cost of $3,260, its historic interest is not only its ornate architecture but also its location near the site of the first sawmill (privately-owned) west of the Mississippi in Minnesota, the Stevens and Tuttle Mill. Only the government sawmill, on the west bank of the river at the site of Minneapolis, preceded the creek mill at Minnetonka Mills.

THE BURWELL HOUSE
AT PRESENT

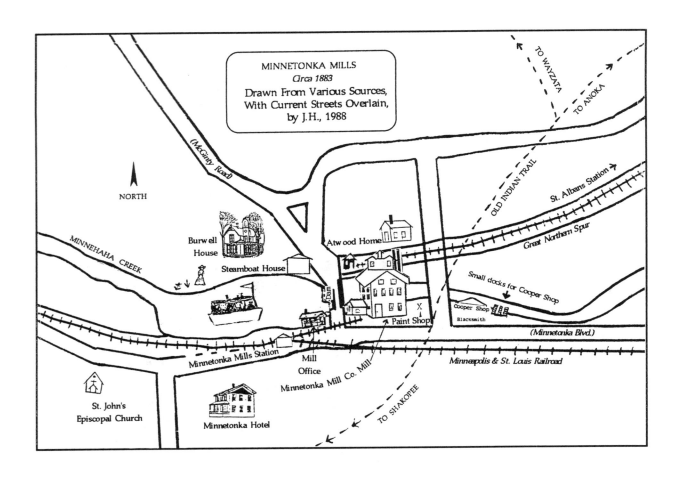

MINNETONKA MILLS
Circa 1883
Drawn From Various Sources,
With Current Streets Overlain,
by J.H., 1988

NORTH

(McGinty Road)

TO WAYZATA

TO ANOKA

OLD INDIAN TRAIL

St. Albans Station →

Great Northern Spur

MINNEHAHA CREEK

Burwell
House

Steamboat House

Atwood Home

Dam

Small docks for Cooper Shop

Cooper Shop

Blacksmith

X

Paint Shop

(Minnetonka Blvd.)

Minnetonka Mills Station

Mill
Office

Minnetonka Mill Co. Mill

Minneapolis & St. Louis Railroad

TO SHAKOPEE

St. John's
Episcopal Church

Minnetonka Hotel

MILL AREA
MINNETONKA
MILLS
1883

The Burwell House is being restored by the City of Minnetonka Historical Society to depict a Victorian home of the 1880s. It is open to the public at specified times and is now on the National Register of Historic Places.

Saturday, June 25, 1988 an ice cream social, open house and antique sale drew a large crowd to the Burwell house and grounds. For a small fee, one could take a self-guided tour through the house. It is beautifully preserved, and the restoration work, historically correct, is nearly completed. Unfortunately, Minnehaha Creek was shallow and green from algae; but the wares of the many antique dealers on the creek's banks distracted the eye from the sorry sight of the creek due to a drought.

Chapter 4

The St. Albans Mill Site

About three-quarters of a mile east of Minnetonka City (Mills), John Alt and Company built a gristmill named St. Albans Mill, in 1874. The mill was south of the present Cedar Lake Road and Mayflower Avenue. It bore the same name as the Great Northern railroad station which was then at Minnetonka City. An old description located the Alt mill "a couple hundred feet above where John Murphy built his house on the island in the creek, where the Terwillegers lived later." Incidentally, a Golden Valley man fondly remembers that there was a popular swimming hole by the Terwilleger house around 1920.

John Alt and his wife, Katie, were from Bavaria, but their four children were born in America. Alt was age forty-four when he started his mill. He had been head miller for the Perkins Mill but left the job when the mill was sold to Messrs. Fletcher and Loring in 1874. Alt's mill was 35 by 45 feet, with three stories and used steel rollers instead of stones for grinding. Due to the steel rollers, it was at one time called Onow, A New Process Mill. Creek waterpower proved insufficient; therefore a thirty horsepower steam engine was installed.

JOHN ALT

During the seven years of its existence, the mill had several owners. Sometimes it was a nuisance to the mill owners back at Minnetonka Mills due to the fact that when the St. Albans gates were closed, water backed up so high at the Minnetonka Mill in the water wheel pit that the wheel would not turn. In 1881 the owners of the Minnetonka Mill Company, purchased the St. Albans Mill from the owner, R. W. Harrison, and dismantled it. The mill turned out quality flour. Even with its brief existence, the St. Albans Mill helped enhance the reputation of the Minnetonka Mills area as a flour-milling center in the 1870s.

Will Perkins, a grandson of the original founder of the Perkins flour mill, said in an interview in 1929 that cattle ran free during the heyday of creek mills and that there were few fences. Cattle would wander up by Alt's mill, with the cowbells on their necks ringing over "a mile or more." He added, "Near Alt's mill was a large and fine patch of wild strawberries. Lady slippers and Indian pinks were thick in the tamarack swamps near the mill."

When canoeing, beware of culverts on the creek in a fast current! To review, and describe the location of one tricky culvert: the creek flows from Minnetonka Mills through Big Willow Park—then to the site of the former St. Albans Mill. The tricky culvert is slightly downstream from there. It is

a rather small culvert under a home access driveway, and if a canoe hits the culvert at a bad angle, such as sideways, the culvert can cause canoe damage. We once saw someone's canoe, damaged irreparably, abandoned there after a battle with the current, and a local man confirmed that it *does* happen.

Today there is a road called St. Albans Mill Road by the creek in

the suburb of Minnetonka, and there is St. Albans Road, West and East, slightly downstream in the suburb of Hopkins. On our history voyage down Minnehaha, we have now passed two of the six former mill sites on the creek where water wheels powered the machinery at the founding of the mills.

Some other culverts to avoid used to be at County Road 73, which is also known as Hopkins Crossroad. A portage is shown on our map around the culverts. Sometimes the culverts could look negotiable at one end but at the other end could be entirely filled with water. However, when we drove down to inspect this spot, we saw that work here the summer of 1987 eliminated the culverts.

Chapter 5

The Stream in St. Louis Park

A bit over one mile east of County Road 73 the creek flows under Minnetonka Boulevard. Here we chose to explore the next three miles of Minnehaha in a two-person rubber boat, propelled, when necessary, by a pole. When the water is shallow and slow, it can take up to three hours to accomplish this float along the sinuosities of the creek. We passed woods, swamps, homes, apartments, the Knollwood Shopping Center, and a building by the creek bridge at Blake Road, where we landed. This section of the creek is popular. As many as forty canoes can be seen going down the creek on a Saturday in the summer when the water level permits it.

THE GLOBE FLOUR MILL---LATER, SCHUSSLER'S MILL

The next place of note ahead on the creek, historically speaking, is at the intersection of Excelsior Boulevard and the creek. Excelsior Boulevard today crosses fairly close to the top of the old mill dam location of the former Globe Flour Mill, built in 1874 at the present Excelsior Boulevard and Minnehaha Creek. The millpond for the mill ran north to south there until about 1898 when the mill was moved, and a new channel was cut through a rise north of the mill site, thus rerouting Minnehaha Creek to its present channel.

1879 MAP

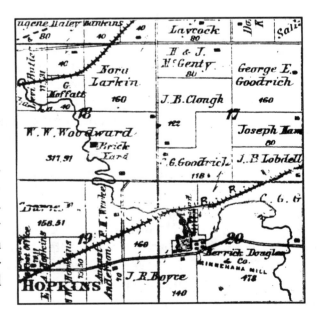

Builders of the mill, which was of frame construction, were William P. Day and Company. Four runs of stone turned out one hundred twenty-five barrels of flour per day. Eighty barrels of this output were daily shipped to a customer in Edinburgh, Scotland under a long-term contract; and the mill also had local and eastern United States customers.

In 1876 the mill sold for nineteen thousand dollars and, in 1879, Jacob K. Sidle bought the mill for twenty-five thousand dollars. Using creek power to turn the water wheel proved inadequate after a few years, and Sidle, Fletcher, Holmes and Co. added a steam engine. This group also built a cooper shop. For shipping and receiving, a side track of the Minneapolis and St. Louis Railroad was used.

Late 1881 saw another change in ownership when Julius Marth and Peter Schussler bought the mill, followed by Schussler's sole ownership in 1882. On an 1884 Hennepin County map, the mill was called Minnehaha Mill. Soon the name was changed to "Schussler's Mill" under Peter Schussler's twelve-year ownership, until 1894.

The mill was taken down in 1898, and the building and original mill-stones were moved to LeSueur Center. No evidence of the mill remains today. A boy who grew up at the mill site became: Otto F. Schussler, M.D.

THE MILLER'S SON

Two little books that Dr. Otto Schussler (the miller's son) published in the 1920s seem to have been inspired by the background of his boyhood years, spent at his father's mill on Minnehaha Creek. The doctor's 1924 book is the story of his brave terrier named "Pills," who held off some attacking, borrowed sled dogs in Alaska and saved the doctor's life. Doctor Schussler fell down while he was driving the dogs and sled on a call, and the terrier protected him until he regained his footing and control of the situation. The book, called *Pills*, also covers other events during the two years that the doctor, his wife, and his dog spent living by gold-bearing Candle Creek in northern Alaska. He dedicated the book to his wife who shared his igloo with him.

Riverside Reveries is the name of Doctor Schussler's 1928 book, a story of the sights he saw around the turn of the century when he worked near the Mississippi in the Fairview and St. Mary's Hospital-Riverside area, including scenes and happenings in Riverside Park. Recalling that Minnehaha Creek was like a little river during his youth, Schussler wrote: "Minnehaha Creek has almost ceased, for a great part of each year at any rate, to be a stream." However, his mental picture of the creek in its glory years remained "fresh and clear as the water that rippled over" its gravel in bygone days.

In both books, the doctor writes about brooks, including Minnehaha, and both have a chapter that relates to Doctor Schussler's boyhood days at Minnehaha Creek, which turned the mill wheel of his father's mill. He gave the location of Schussler's Mill as one mile east of Hopkins station on what is now Excelsior Boulevard.

The doctor's mill memories were of the millpond swimming hole; the semi-dark inside of the mill, caused by paste on the window panes and dust in the air; the purr of the millstones and the "unforgettable gristmill odor." He wrote that the spray from a foaming waterfall, like that by a mill, gave an "olfactory stimulus" and described a spring bubbling out of rock as "living water."

A bit of his philosophy about brooks:

> Everyone, almost without exception...loves a brook...I suspect that it can be explained partly thus—here at last is a creature (for it surely is a live thing, else how could it sing so sweetly and talk and laugh and dance and run? Tell me that!)...Yes, we say here is a creature that has the spirit and the courage and the good sense, too, to follow its own inclinations...Do you wonder after all, when its merits are disclosed, that it touches the soul of each and all and finds a place in every heart?

The creek meanders from the suburb of Minnetonka into Hopkins (and back); then it flows into St. Louis Park and through a corner of Hopkins and back into St. Louis Park, which loses it to Edina for a short distance and grabs it back, only to lose it again to Edina.

Towards the southern borders of St. Louis Park, Minnehaha widens into Meadowbrook Lake, or Pond. This lake was named in June, 1925. In 1929 Meadowbrook Lake was excavated to increase it to twenty acres, with an average depth of ten feet. Fill from the lake was used on the public golf course which surrounds the lake. Woodchucks, or groundhogs, are often seen on shore here as well as an occasional raccoon.

MEADOWBROOK LAKE

Nearby resident, Mark Ennenga, president of the Creekside Chapter of the Izaak Walton League in 1980, said in a *Sun* newspaper interview (August, 1980) that his chapter yearly had been cleaning the creek from Minnetonka to Minneapolis. The 1979 cleanup received recognition as the best in the nation by the Izaak Walton League. Debris that year nearly filled two dump trucks. Nevertheless, the creek has nurtured Ennenga's love of nature, and he told the *Sun* reporter:

IZAAK WALTON LEAGUE

> I've gotten into nature a lot more since I came back from Vietnam. That's because I feel I'm alive today because of nature. If you knew what to look for you could tell if there was an enemy containment in the swamp ahead. If there are people hanging out there, the birds don't act the same. I can say personally that the animals tipped me off to an ambush a couple of times. [He still is a bird watcher.] I'm at the creek all the time. This is really one of the wildest parts of the city. There are parts of this creek I could take you to and you'd think you were one hundred miles out of town...We just have to make sure that future generations see the creek as we've seen it.

In an August, 1988 phone conversation, Ennenga said that the Izaak

Walton League Creekside Chapter has adopted the St. Louis Park creek portion where it flows through St. Louis Park, and they call it a "Save our Stream Program." It is a permanent adoption program under the national Izaak Walton League. Ennenga also mentioned that in many places along the route of Minnehaha Creek it is still a wild creek, but in other places it turns into a *civilized* creek channel that is maintained. The question is—at what point of civilizing it do you lose the creek and its refuges for wildlife?

HUGE
CREEK
SNAPPING
TURTLE

The head was four inches long and its body was about sixteen inches in diameter.

Chapter 6

Sampling the Edina Part of the Creek

On the west side of Highway 100, near the man-made Edina Cascade structure on the creek, a blue heron was spotted in 1988. That year, also, egrets were seen making their home under the Highway 100 bridge.

There is a very important portage at the Old Millpond by Browndale Avenue in Edina where there is a dam and a waterfall of about fifteen feet which falls with a lot of force. Another way to identify this portage is that it is on the north side of Fiftieth Street, opposite the Edina Country Club.

The dam and falls at this spot illustrate the waterpower used for the mill built here in 1857. John Marriott, a carpenter and farmer who worked on the mill, was paid for his labor with a cow, by Captain Strout. The mill and its site belonged to four men in 1857—Jacob Elliot, Richard Strout, Levi M. Stewart and Joseph Cushman.

The mill was sold in January, 1859, to Jonathan T. Grimes and William C. Rheem and named the "Waterville Mill." During the Civil War, the army at Fort Snelling ordered flour from the mill, and men searched the **WATERVILLE MILL** countryside to get enough wheat to operate the mill day and night. Allen Baird, the son of one of the Richfield mill owners, was one of the millers. Owner Grimes was not a miller, but he kept the books and hauled flour to the fort with his team of horses, the first team in the area. Grimes trusted his horses to know the way home from the fort while he grabbed a rare chance to sleep—in the bottom of the wagon.

Daniel Buckwalter bought the mill in 1867 and named it the Buckwalter Mill. Also known as The Red Mill, the name that lasted was "Edina Mills."

At first the mill was an old fashioned gristmill. It was a two-story building which measured 40 by 36 feet, with a heavy timber frame, assembled by placing a projecting piece of one timber into the slot of another and fastening the two timbers together with a wooden peg. Most beams were hand hewn, and some of the timbers were eighteen-feet long. Some timbers used were made from oak trees cut in the woods near the mill. The outside had a wood-shingle roof and vertical siding boards twelve-inches wide, with wooden strips covering the joints.

In 1869, Andrew Craik bought the mill and named it "Edina Mills" after **ANDREW CRAIK**

his birthplace, Edinburgh, Scotland. During the latter half of the 1800s Andrew Craik and members of his family were prominent in the village that came to be known as Edina and in the city of Minneapolis. Born in 1817, he came to Canada with his parents when he was only one year old. As a young man, he was in the milling business in Canada, and at about age forty-four, he owned a flour mill in LaCrosse, Wisconsin. Al-

though prospering, he sought more opportunity in Minneapolis; and he promised his four sons that he would set them up in business if they joined him in the move. The family lived at the corner of Nicollet Avenue and Eighth Street before Craik bought the mill.

William, the oldest son, became owner of a ladies' drygoods store on Washington Avenue, kittycorner from the Nicollet House; the second son, James, became a civil engineer who surveyed railroad lines and the streetcar line to Minnetonka during his career. The third son, John, operated the Edina mill and a dairy farm on the site of today's Edina Country Club golf course. The fourth son, Alexander, handled the retail flour mill and feed store in downtown Minneapolis, which was the usual way to find outlets for the miller's tenth of the grain processed and other products. The Craik's large house and grounds occupied the southwest corner of the present Fiftieth Street and Wooddale, by Minnehaha Creek—the site of an Edina park today. Besides the four sons, the Craiks were also blessed with one daughter.

Craik's mill prospered, and the bridge by his mill was one of only three bridges across the creek for a while. Both factors helped make several locations at what today is Fiftieth Street between France Avenue and Highway 100 blossom into community and business centers. For instance, a rural village grew up around the mill, and eventually there was a school, church, blacksmith and, later, a post office and store. The Grange Hall, which was the first headquarters for the Village of Edina, was built east of the mill in 1879 at the present Wooddale Avenue and Fiftieth Street, on the site now occupied by St. Stephen's Episcopal Church.

Under the ownership of Andrew Craik and his son, John, a brick kiln for browning or roasting oats and a sandstone oat huller were installed to make oatmeal, a product inspired by Craik's Scottish heritage. The mill's specialty became the manufacture of oatmeal and pearl barley. This was the first mill to turn out these products in Hennepin County. The waterpower from the fifteen-foot fall of the creek turned one thirty-six-inch and two thirty-inch turbine water wheels which furnished fifty horsepower. At this period, the mill's capacity was ten to twelve barrels

a day. Two millstones were used for flour and one for feed.

George Millam was hired as the miller at Edina Mills beginning in 1869. He was known as the Edina Miller. In a 1924 *Minneapolis Journal* interview, Millam pointed to some golfers across the street from the old mill, at the Edina Country Club, and said they were at the spot where the Dakota Indians under Chief Shakopee set up their tepees while waiting for the mill to grind their grain.

In the 1924 interview, George Millam said he used to see lots of fish in the creek and many deer and wolves in the woods. The mill was to the right of the bridge at Browndale and Minnehaha Creek, as you face north.

BROWNDALE

Wealthy cattleman Henry F. Brown bought the Edina Mill property around 1892. He owned a farm called Browndale Farm, which adjoined the mill property, and he changed the name to "Browndale Mill." There was little water in the creek at the time, shutting the mill down, at least for a while. "The mill ceased manufacturing flour at the turn of the century but continued to grind feed until World War I," according to the Edina Historical Society in a report on their summer, 1977, Edina mill excavation project.

People from many parts of the world were drawn to the creek vicinity on the Browndale Farm to see or buy cattle from Brown's famous herd of Shorthorns. Brown was the uncle of Sheriff Earle Brown, who founded the Minnesota Highway Patrol. Known as a breeder of fine cattle, Henry Brown became one of the most prominent breeders of Shorthorns in the

United States. One of his Shorthorns was the sweepstakes prize winner at the 1893 Chicago World's Fair, and for years his Shorthorns won first place at any state fair where he chose to exhibit them. Other involvements of this creekside resident were in lumber, banking, flour milling, telegraphy and the Minneapolis Street Railway. Brown's wife, Susan, was a member of the 1893 World's Fair commission for Minnesota and also helped manage the women's department at that fair.

HENRY BROWN LIVESTOCK AD, 1883

In their *History of Minneapolis and Hennepin County, Minnesota* (1914) Holcombe and Bingham note the fame of the creekside farm:

Visitors from many parts of the world have been to Browndale to see the famous herd and attend the annual Browndale auction of Shorthorns, and the Browndale strain has representatives wherever men value high-bred and superior livestock. So many notable animals have been bred on this farm that its output figures with great prominence in the pedigree records in this country and abroad.

Henry F. Brown, native of Maine, went down in Minnesota history as, among many other accomplishments, the man who pushed for the name "Edina." At a Grange Hall meeting in 1888 the name of "Westfield" was approved for the little village near the mill. Henry Brown objected, campaigned fast for the name "Edina," and it won by a vote of 47 to 42. He is also remembered because Browndale Avenue in Edina is named after his farm.

Construction of the Grays Bay dam in 1897 was one of the things that led to the decline of the Edina Mills because of less waterpower. Auxiliary power was added; but competition from the giant mills in Minneapolis was too great, and the old Edina mill was torn down in 1932.

In 1922 Thorpe Bros. Realty Company bought the site of the Edina mill and Browndale Farm from Henry Brown's estate. Along with some of the adjoining George W. Baird land, the property became the well-planned and desirable community called the Edina Country Club District. Minnehaha Creek enlivens many a back yard on the west side of the Country Club today as the creek's appearance, vegetation and wildlife population change with the seasons.

Dwight Williams Park is at the Edina mill site today near the fifteen-foot waterfall. The little park features a memorial display of the mill in honor of Williams, who was an Edina resident killed in action April 30, 1945 during World War II.

DWIGHT
WILLIAMS

MAP MEMORIES
Circa 1890s

Note that Henry Brown owned land on both sides of the creek. Brown's neighbor, James A. Bull, bought a milk route, and the family peddled sixty gallons a day to as far away as Seventh Street in downtown Minneapolis.

Bull's son, Coates P. Bull, wrote that Henry Brown's champion Shorthorn cattle gave a lot of milk "in those days," but their milk supply diminished greatly when other breeders bred them for beef.

Birds and animals C. P. Bull listed as being along the creek when they had their farm there were: American osprey (fish hawks), which nested in the creek's banks, and mink, otters and muskrats, which built their dens along the banks.

Circa 1880s

To the north on the map is the J. T. Grimes property in 1898. Grimes' daughter, Ella Alma Grimes Eustis, wrote an article called "Out of My Mind," which the Edina Historical Society has in its archives. Some things she mentions about Minnehaha Creek are: a sampler with a wood frame on which small shells from the creek had been embedded in putty, to make a design; crosses made of shells; and the times when she and other small children baited hooks with angleworms and caught sunfish or catfish at the creek. Their large dining room served,in winter, as a bedroom, kitchen and sitting room. In winter, the cookstove was moved in there for heat and cooking. When Ella had a cold, she found it pleasant to "crawl into that warm bed in the dining room and cover up with nice, clean buffalo robes." Inside, wood shutters served for storm

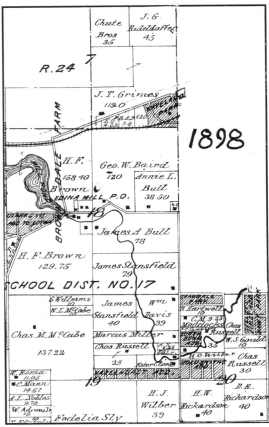

EDINA POST OFFICE
BROWNDALE FARM

THORIS ROACH
AND
LYLE SMITH
WITH
HOMEMADE
BOATS, 1912

windows; and mosquito netting was tacked up each summer on the outside first-floor windows to serve as screens. She did not recall netting on the second floor windows as mosquitos were not supposed to be able to fly that high.

They traded beef for parts of hogs to make ham and bacon in their smokehouse; and they obtained mutton from the George Bairds, their neighbors. To water their cattle, Ella's brother, Melvin, preferred driving the cows over to Minnehaha Creek, less than a mile away. This was easier than drawing a lot of water from their well. He liked to ride one of the young steers and race with other boys over to the creek as they drove the cattle. Late in the fall, one of the fat, young steers would be butchered, quartered and hung up to freeze for the family's winter supply of beef.

A two-story building was built about fifty feet from the Grimes house to store wood, and one end was "filled with ice from Minnehaha Creek, packed in sawdust," Ella recalled. Upstairs, the family stored chicken feed, and one end was used as a lovely playhouse where Ella played with her dolls, Lillie, Nellie and Rosie.

From the Edina mill memorial park, the creek passes under Fiftieth Street and flows by the Edina Country Club golf course and tennis courts and park land—then near the foundation of a huge, stone church, St. Stephens Episcopal Church, where a church secretary once said that it is very pleasant and soothing to look out the windows at the rippling creek. After passing through an Edina neighborhood, the creek offers a portage at West Fifty-fourth Street. The water can run fast here, and it is necessary to portage as mapped. There is a huge culvert-type passageway, with a bend in it, under the bridge at France Avenue. This is the area at what is now Fifty-Seventh and France and the creek, where two Clark sons had homes from 1884 to past the turn of the century. Their mother, Esther Clark, wrote some stories in her diary about their life there.

MAP MEMORIES
Circa 1880s

THE CLARK FAMILY

L. L. Clark and Esther Clark, in turn, owned property on Minnehaha Creek at its most southern winding in the present Edina, starting in the 1880s. The property was at first part of Richfield and, later, part of Edina. Clark ownership is known to be as early as 1884 and as late as 1913. Two of John and Esther Clark's sons had homes on the property, and one of the sons, Fred, had a blacksmith shop there. The senior Clark, John, owned Hennepin Carriage Works, 1502 Hennepin Avenue, a carriage-making and blacksmith shop, which John opened in about 1876.

While engaged in a genealogical search, Mrs. Clark's great-great-granddaughter found some of Esther Clark's writings in Missouri. Preserved by a woman relative, age ninety-nine, the gold mine of memories contained stories Mrs. Clark penned about her married sons and their families who lived on the creek at what is today in the vicinity of Fifty-seventh Street and France Avenue South and Minnehaha Creek. The house sites appear on this 1890 Hennepin County map.

Little Eva, the oldest grandchild of the Clark creek clan, stars in the stories. A condensed version follows:

AT THE SITE OF THE PRESENT

FIFTY-SEVENTH STREET AND MINNEHAHA CREEK

The pretty little home of Fred and Lizzie Clark was in a grove of trees, and the view from the front of the house was of a footbridge over beautiful Minnehaha Creek. "The dooryard extended down to the little river where Eva [the oldest child, born about 1878] used to wade and play and frighten me out of my wits when I was there, for fear she would be drowned," wrote grandma Esther Clark. Grandma continued, "Here too she had a swing and a hammock under the tall shady trees, and her Papa made her a pretty, rustic seat, and her Mama planted flowers so she had a lovely place to play with her little sister and cousins that lived nearby." Little Eva and her Mama liked to pick wild plums; also, they loved to gather wildflowers to decorate the table in front of the double windows in their parlor.

CLARK HOUSES AT
SOUTHERN BEND
OF THE CREEK
1890

Eva often went to play *up* at the nearby home of her Uncle Luther (Lute) and family. "The house was on a hill in a lovely grove where you could look down and see the winding Minnehaha shining out and in among the drooping willows that grew along the shore. The loveliest flowers grew all over the hillside and way down in the meadow," wrote Grandma.

THE BROKEN ARM

One day when little Eva was about two years old, she climbed down the steps of the small porch on her house and ran through the fields. A short distance from the house, one of her father's horses either stepped on her arm, or kicked her, and her arm was broken below the elbow. Her Mama carried her, crying and screaming, over to the house of a neighbor, a Mrs. Davis. Soon Eva's father came and, looking at the arm, knew he must take the long horse and buggy ride to Minneapolis and get a doctor to come and ease his daughter's pain for the night. The next day they took Eva to live in town with grandma and grandpa for a while so the physician could see her every day. The doctor came to the grandparents' house and put on a cast of "pieces of board and plaster of Paris...she had to hold it just one way for

ESTHER (PALMER) CLARK
1830-1911

three weeks," Mrs. Clark remembered. When the doctor took the smooth, narrow boards off, Eva's arm had mended fine. Grandma Esther saved the splint boards and painted some strawberries and vines on one board and apple blossoms on the other. Grandma hung them on a ribbon so Eva could see them every day.

Esther Clark described her grandchild, Eva, as a bright little girl, with yellow hair, rosy cheeks and sky-blue eyes. She was a strong child and helped her Mama with the care of her baby sister, Jessie.

THE FIVE LITTLE PIGS

One pleasant summer afternoon, baby Jessie somehow got up from her nap and went out the back door onto the stoop. Just then, five squealing, hungry, little pigs escaped from their pen behind the house and ran up the hill toward the open door and the baby. Grandma Esther wrote about the melee that followed:

On they came [the pigs], straight for baby and the house...in they went, looked about, [and] not finding anything to eat, started for baby again. Baby began to cry and Eva to scream and caught up sticks and stones and threw at them and tried as much as she could to drive them away.

They came nearer and nearer, at last were so close they caught baby's dress in their mouths, and poor little Eva...stood her ground and kicked and pounded...calling at the top of her voice for her Mama and Uncle Luther who, as good luck would have it, was at home and heard her and ran as fast as he could, and just as he reached them, one of the pigs caught one of baby's hands in its mouth...The sight of Uncle Lute with a club and the noise he and Eva made together frightened the pig so much it dropped the little bruised hand, but not before the blood had started. They all scampered off down the hill to their pen, which wind or something had broken down, and that is the reason they were running wild...She [Eva] was frightened almost to death, but she would not leave little Jessie alone with the pigs. So I am sure she was the means of saving her sister's life.

As a young woman, Eva married, but her short life had a tragic ending. She contracted typhoid in her twenties; circumstances delayed medical care, and she died. The illness was probably not related to creek waters as she did not live near the creek at that time.

THE WYMAN FAMILY

The house shown here was at a site, in 1898, on Minnehaha Creek, about two short blocks downstream from the location of the Clark home just described. This was the home of the Gustav H. Wyman family at the time. It was on the south side of the creek between what is now Ewing and Drew

GUSTAV H. WYMAN HOUSE BETWEEN EWING AND DREW, EDINA, 1898

Avenues South at Fifty-seventh Street, on land that was part of the old Hawthorne Farm, acreage of 540 acres, which included quite a bit of shoreline along the most southern windings of Minnehaha Creek in Edina. One of the Wyman descendants suggested that this house was old in 1898 and is quite likely the original Hawthorne farmhouse, as there is a mark for the house on Section 20 of an 1879 Hennepin County map. The house site marked is set back a bit from the creek [on a hill] and the old map shows a little access road that came to the house from what became France Avenue.

Gustav Wyman's descendants, Edwin, Jennie and Leland, talked about their family being part of the story of Minnehaha Creek in an interview on April 7, 1990. Edwin, talking about his family, said:

> My folks came to the U.S.A. from Sweden in 1893. My oldest sister, Esther, was born in Sweden and was about three months old when they came to America on the steamship *Alaska*.
>
> This picture was taken about 1898. This is where my parents lived on the [former] Hawthorne Farm...Note the American flag displayed on the porch. My folks were extremely patriotic and proud to be living in America. On the porch is my mother, Emma Wyman, holding my sister, Anna. Standing beside her is my sister, Ella. Seated is my father, Gustav H. Wyman, and with him is my oldest sister, Esther.
>
> I do not know who the other two men are in the picture. In early days, often the milk delivery man lived with the farmers where the milk was produced.

By 1910, the Gustav Wyman family had moved to western Edina where they rented a house on the Will Ryan farm, Valley View Road. When that farm was sold, they bought, in 1921, a house nearby, which later was assigned the address of 5320 Valley View Road. This spot was in the path of the future Sixty-second Street Crosstown Highway. The house was built by a Minneapolis lumber dealer in 1905 as a country retreat, and the large tile bricks for the fireplace came from Italy. In 1964, the family paid $5,000 to move the house to Chanhassen to make way for the Sixty-second Street freeway, and the Leland Wyman family now lives in it.

WYMAN AVENUE

Wyman Avenue in Edina is named for this family, as well as a bridge named "Wyman" over the Crosstown Highway. Edwin Wyman contributed a piece of land there.

Two of Gustav Wyman's children, Edwin and Jennie Wyman Smith, recalled highlights of school life when they attended the Edina school, on Fiftieth Street, near Minnehaha Creek, circa 1910-18. The Edina City Hall is on its site today.

Jennie said:

> Children walked to the Edina school in early fall and late spring; but "school rigs" picked us up in cold weather, on a regular route. The rigs were heavy farm

Edina School. 1908

wagons and sleighs, covered with canvas like a covered wagon, and drawn by two horses. The driver put bedding straw on the floor to help warm the children's feet in the winter. When there was no snow for the sleigh, it took a big stretch of our legs to climb up on the farm wagon instead of the lower sleigh.

EDINA
GRADE SCHOOL
*Courtesy
Leland Wyman*

The Edina school was built in 1888 and it was of tan brick. About 1915 the school was enlarged to an eight-room building, with the addition in the form of a second story. At that time the "Boys" and "Girls" outside bathroom facilities were replaced with chemical toilets.

There were two big rooms in the school's basement, which had a base of poured concrete. The girls had one room and the boys another for indoor play at recesses during inclement weather. One room had a small kitchen area. To end outdoor morning and afternoon recesses, the teacher rang a hand bell, and the kids came running towards the school. There was no kindergarten class—only first through eighth grades.

Bag lunch supplements were made down in the basement of the Edina grade school. The children brought their lunches, and a Mrs. Culver made unforgettable delicious cocoa in a gigantic granite kettle for them. Sometimes she made tasty vegetable soup, too. School ran from eight-thirty in the morning to four in the afternoon. After school, kids would often run down the hill and head for Rorrison's Ma and Pa store across the iron bridge, from which they could see the Edina mill and hear the noise of the

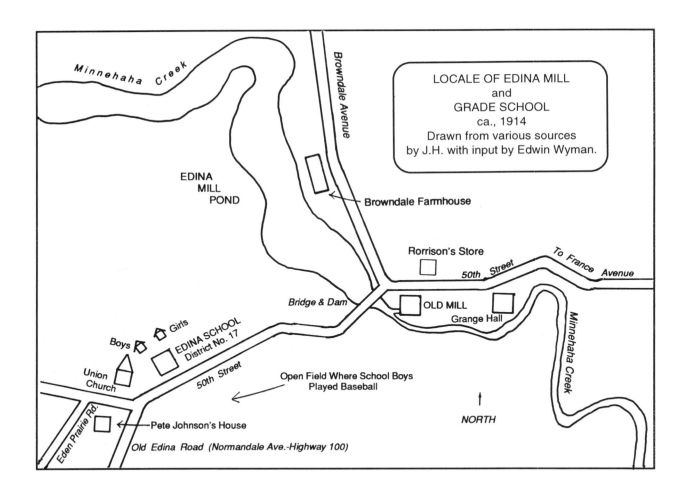

LOCALE OF EDINA MILL
and
GRADE SCHOOL
ca., 1914
Drawn from various sources
by J.H. with input by Edwin Wyman.

Minnehaha Creek

Browndale Avenue

EDINA
MILL
POND

Browndale Farmhouse

Rorrison's Store

50th Street

To France Avenue

Bridge & Dam

OLD MILL

Grange Hall

Minnehaha Creek

Girls

Boys

EDINA SCHOOL
District No. 17

Union
Church

50th Street

Open Field Where School Boys
Played Baseball

Eden Prairie Rd.

NORTH

Pete Johnson's House

Old Edina Road (Normandale Ave.-Highway 100)

waterfall right where it is today. Ed Wyman says that circa 1917, Fiftieth ran east and west over the mill dam, and the Edina mill was on the south side of Fiftieth, while Rorrison's store was on the north side of Fiftieth. When one went into the store, a bell rang to bring one of the storekeepers from their living quarters. "At that time, you could get a penny's worth of candy," recalled Ed Wyman.

Up to the fourth grade, Ed wore knickers to school. His sister Jennie recalled, "In 1930, I wore my first slacks on vacation, a two-piece suit of white duck, with sailor-type collar and bell-bottom slacks. Of course, we did *not* wear slacks to school!"

There was a great big field across from the school—Henry Brown's land—that the school used as a baseball field. Boys usually played just two official games each year, one against Lake Harriet school and one against Robert Fulton school, with an added competition, a few times, against a St. Paul school. Right about on top of the baseball field, the first Edina Country Club building was built close to Fiftieth Street. It burned, was rebuilt and later built on Wooddale Avenue. Normandale Road (Highway 100) was called the Edina Road.

Jennie remembered a cheer they used in school competitions at the baseball field:

> Edina, Edina!
> You did well!
> Robert Fulton!
> Go to hell!!

Ed remembered the cheer:

> Skinny Minneapolis!
> Fat St. Paul!
> Edina, Edina!
> The best of all!!

Edwin's son, Leland Wyman, attended Wooddale grade school near Minnehaha Creek, Edina, and Edina High School. Built in 1926, Wooddale was torn down in 1985; and its predecessor, the little Edina grade school, was torn down in the 1920s.

THE HIAWATHA FESTIVAL

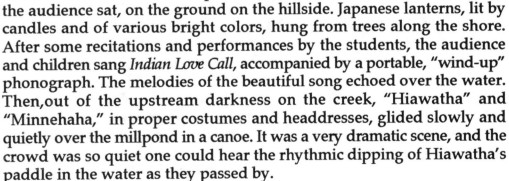

One year, about 1917, the Edina grade school held a Hiawatha Festival in the evening, at the Edina millpond. Students who were in fourth grade up to eighth grade participated, and Ed Wyman was among them.

There was a beautiful, wooded hill on the west bank of the creek at the Edina millpond, and that is where the audience sat, on the ground on the hillside. Japanese lanterns, lit by candles and of various bright colors, hung from trees along the shore. After some recitations and performances by the students, the audience and children sang *Indian Love Call*, accompanied by a portable, "wind-up" phonograph. The melodies of the beautiful song echoed over the water. Then, out of the upstream darkness on the creek, "Hiawatha" and "Minnehaha," in proper costumes and headdresses, glided slowly and quietly over the millpond in a canoe. It was a very dramatic scene, and the crowd was so quiet one could hear the rhythmic dipping of Hiawatha's paddle in the water as they passed by.

MILL SITE PRESERVATION

In a unique project for the Bicentennial, the old mill site was excavated through efforts of the Edina Historical Society and Edina government. Many facts about the mill were uncovered, from old bottles to engineering details of machinery and the mill foundations. The story and drawings

DWIGHT WILLIAMS PARK (Edina Mill Site) The blocks outline the mill. Millstones were superimposed and the top one, the RUNNER STONE, was driven by a shaft from the waterwheel. It rotated against the bottom one, the BED STONE. Grain was poured into the center, the EYE, and the ground grain (flour) worked its way to the outside through the grooves in the stones.

from the dig are in a booklet, *Report on the Excavation of the Edina Mill, Summer, 1977,* by Richard R. Busch and the Edina Historical Society. Now the mill site and other features of the old mill are marked on the grounds with lumber and stone.

BROWNDALE FARM

Henry Brown's home near the creek and the mill was an especially nice place. It had a big front porch to the east and a porch on the south side, also. It faced Browndale Avenue, which was "dedicated," or laid out, by Henry Brown; and the farmhouse and farm yard were in the semi-circle formed at present by Browndale and Edgebrook Place, near 46th and Browndale. The one and one-half story house had beamed ceilings and woodwork carved out of several types of wood.

The Brown's main residence was in Minneapolis. At the turn of the century, they entertained their friends at the farm for a Fourth-of-July celebration. French chefs from a Minneapolis hotel prepared picnic lunches and ice cream for the guests.

Henry Brown had a platform built in his yard by Minnehaha Creek where his guests danced a hoe-down to the tunes of an orchestra. When McCrory's Motor Line was extended from Lake Harriet to Excelsior, the Browns gave a party, and all guests came out on the new line.

Chapter 7

Childhood by Minnehaha Creek
in the 1920s and 1930s
Personal Account by Jane King Hallberg

Paddling on down the creek, beyond the site of the Wyman farm, we see a little bridge over the stream, and the banks are quite woodsy. Back by France Avenue, we passed a cemetery that has been there for many years. At York and Xerxes Avenues, the beginning of City of Minneapolis park property, roads and parkways follow the creek most of the way to the creek's mouth, which is about seven miles ahead.

Minnehaha Creek and its valley from York Avenue to Washburn Avenue South contain some of the best recreational space on the entire creek's length. Of course, I love this area because this is where I grew up.

SUMMER

In my neighborhood around York Avenue, the creek was usually about two feet deep and about twenty feet wide. There was a sandy bottom and a gentle current of crystal clear water. By the bridge on Xerxes Avenue, it deepened a bit into what is remembered as an old swimmin' hole of the early 1900s where boys would sometimes swim in the buff when they had the place to themselves. By 1927, there was wading near Xerxes but not much swimming. Parents warned it might be polluted from cesspools and other drainage as sewers did not go into the streets in this area until about 1930. Instead of swimming, there was another attraction by the creek bridge on Xerxes— the "crick" store.

A CRICK STORE REGULAR IN 1928 The Author in a boyish-bob with spit curls.

THE "CRICK" STORE

There used to be a little store in a tan, stucco bungalow beside Minnehaha Creek at Fifty-fourth and Xerxes Avenue South in the 1920s and 1930s. We children went to the Crick Store on errands and were usually given one cent or more for a treat. Kids came streaming to the store like ants to sweets. Most children came barefoot, but the owners did not object. Only about one-fourth of the tan, stucco bungalow was the store, and it was on the crick side of the house. The dominant fixture in the store to us was a six-foot-wide slanted candy case with a display of such goodies as licorice or white-chalky candy cigarettes, fluted tin pans containing pink or white sticky candy pies, varicolored candy dots stuck on a long paper streamer, round all-day suckers, and brown caramel "all-week" suckers.

Two different families ran the store over the years. All the storekeepers were patient and picked out a penny's worth of one candy and two cents' worth of another and put it in a small, brown bag for their delighted child customers.

At times we watched the flow of the creek from the bridge as we chewed caramels or smoked our candy cigarettes—or we sat on the grassy banks of the creek as we munched candy and talked and talked and talked.

VISITORS TO THE CREEK NEIGHBORHOOD

Many vendors, who came around regularly, added interest and color to our creek neighborhood. It was a transition time between horse-drawn vehicles and automobiles in the twenties and early thirties. Therefore, some vendors used horses and some drove cars or trucks. At Fifty-third and York Avenue South, we lived on the southern city limits of Minneapolis. Just across Minnehaha Creek there were only a few scattered houses and farms; yet, many salesmen came to our area.

THE ICEMAN

One vendor who came often was the ice man, Mr. Day. He chopped blocks of ice to order. While he carried the block ice, over his back, to the customer's icebox, children reached into the wagon or truck bed for chips of ice. Other frequent vendors were the Bambi man, with bread, jelly rolls and other bakery products; and the popcorn man, who dispensed popcorn in white bags, dripping with butter, for five cents and ten cents. The popcorn man's white, box-like, glassed-in cart, his horse, and the shrill automatic whistle insured attention and popularity. The beverage and spice man came less frequently. He sold a delicious nectar base and the base for root beer. The latter, in our family, was mixed in a white porcelain baby's bathtub. Then the root beer was bottled and set aside to work.

The milkman in our area came very early. A card in our window provided the milk order, and a metal box was provided to hold the milk for the convenience of the customer. I remember the milk was not homogenized, and the three inches of cream in the glass bottle was poured off for coffee and other uses.

THE DOUGHNUT MAN

During the Depression years, a doughnut man came door-to-door to sell delicious, crispy, homemade doughnuts. His wife made the doughnuts, and the little business enabled the couple to scrape by in those hard times.

Periodically, the junk man would appear, with his old horse clopping along, pulling a wooden wagon full of household discards. It must have been after Prohibition ended in 1933 that the junk man gave the folks two bottles of sweet, red, homemade wine. I'll never forget that our folks gave, or sold, our 1920s Lionel train to the junk man!

HORSE VISITORS

Two runaway workhorses crossed Minnehaha Creek and invaded our small garden one day. We saw them feasting on our corn, and from behind our screen door the horse thieves looked monstrous. It was an educated guess that their owner was Mr. Danen. Our parents knew him because he and his horses and plow had excavated for the basement of our 1922-built home; so they called Mr. Danen at his home. I do not know for sure that the horses belonged to Danen; but soon a man, clad in overalls, appeared. He took control of the horses, heading them south on Xerxes Avenue, across the creek bridge, to their barn.

A few times some of the York Avenue gang of girls tried camping in a backyard near the creek—either under a blanket draped over a low clothesline and staked down or in an old umbrella-type tent. As the night grew darker, sounds in the distance, such as dogs howling or bullfrogs croaking at the creek, became in our imagination the howls of wolves and the snorts of bears. Escorted by a disgruntled "host" father, we headed home to our own comfortable beds. I once survived the night alone in a regular tent when my fellow camper became ill; and she, Marilyn, went home in the middle of the night without waking anyone.

THE YORK AVENUE GANG

On some fine summer days we set out on expeditions to explore the creek, usually downstream. There were houses set back from the creek in many places, but we ignored these signs of civilization and penetrated the wilderness along Minnehaha to the east as far as Penn Avenue, which was about ten short blocks from our homes. Sometimes our goal was to hike the seven miles to Minnehaha Falls, but we never accomplished it.

Our trip to Penn Avenue could take hours as we looked for clams, fish, frogs and turtles—waded—threw stones in creek waters—or discussed a gang of neighborhood boys. We feared and admired the boys and sometimes played softball in the street with them. Once we crossed the creek to their "fort" which was a 7 by 7 foot sandy hole, about five-feet deep. In fact, the whole neighborhood was sandy, including the creek. The gang's hideout was on the south creek bank opposite York Avenue in a hillside and covered with boards. Caves could not be safely dug in this soil. The "B." gang was not there, as we well knew when we approached. We jumped in and out of the fort and ran away fast. The worst these tough guys ever did was push us down in a cinder-paved alley during a game of *Run, sheep, run.*

FORMER CASCADE
ON MINNEHAHA
AT PENN AVENUE
1880s
*Courtesy
Hennepin
History Museum*

An 1880 picture I discovered shows a waterfall of ten feet or more at Penn Avenue on the creek. It was not there in the 1920s or 1930s; but the creek drops there today, with an increase in the current. After the so-called two hundred year rainstorm and flood of July, 1987, I saw two women, each holding a child, floating on inner tubes, as they sped under the Penn Avenue bridge and along the flooded creek and parkways beside it.

"The records show that in 1894...the [park] department carried out some creekbed corrections," wrote Theodore Wirth in his book, *Minneapolis Park System, 1883-1944.*

In an unpublished article about Minnetonka Mills and its schools, Louise Burwell tells about an *1851* trip up Minnehaha Creek, via boat, by Simon Stevens and Calvin Tuttle. This must have been a word of mouth story she heard when she lived at Minnetonka Mills for so many years. She wrote that the men portaged around Minnehaha Falls and traveled up the creek until they reached a "rushing and leaping cascade...Over the banks, hung the branches of the oak and elm, intermingled with the red

RED CEDAR
LANE

cedar." [This cascade was quite likely the falls in the picture, at Penn Avenue, as even today there are red cedar trees in the area, and for years there has been a "Red Cedar Lane" slightly upstream from Penn Avenue near the creek at about Upton Avenue.]

Stevens and Tuttle considered putting a sawmill at the cascade, but their Indian friends urged them on to the big lake (Minnetonka) where they saw lots of timber and the rapids at the site of Minnetonka Mills "where the water rushed so forcibly and so beautifully over the rocks," Louise wrote. They explored part of the lake at the creek inlet and returned to the site of their proposed sawmill.

The importance of Miss Burwell's story in regard to Minnehaha Creek is that it reveals a second natural waterfall on the creek in the 1800s. (The Edina waterfall appears to be a result of the man-made mill dam.)

Recently, I met a man, Wyllys McElroy, who lived on "my" block a few years before I did. When he was about eight years old, McElroy's dad rented a farm and farmhouse at the southwest end of Fifty-third and York. The two-story, light yellow house was at the top of the hill by Minnehaha Creek. I remember the farmhouse, although the McElroys lived there about 1914-18, and my folks built our house at the other end of the block in 1922. Wyllys' family rented from Preacher W. B. Riley, pastor of the First Baptist Church in downtown Minneapolis. The farm consisted of ten acres of land along the creek, where the McElroys raised cows and chickens. Wyllys' dad went by horse and wagon on a milk route and also sold chickens. **WYLLYS McELROY**

City water service was available in the area by 1922 but not sewer service. The McElroy farmhouse had outside bathroom facilities and a pump and well. However, houses built around 1922 and after in that block had inside bathrooms. The farmhouse burned down in the late 1920s or early 1930s and was empty at the time.

East of France Avenue, along the creek, boys played at what they called the sand banks, and they swam in the creek there near Beard Avenue South. Wyllys McElroy remembers a dairy farm on the northwest corner of France, at Fifty-fourth. The creek ran through it. Another great swimmin' hole was at a bend in the creek by York Avenue where young Wyllys learned to swim.

There used to be a so-called hermit who lived at about Fifty-fifth and the creek on the west side of France Avenue, opposite the cemetery. In about 1938 I went with a carload of teenagers on an adventure that was supposed to be spooky—visiting the hermit. We drove into his narrow road and back to his house near Minnehaha Creek; and a man with a beard, the hermit, came out and politely talked with us for a while. Beards were not common in those post-World War I military-oriented days, and this must have been the reason that the bachelor became known as a hermit. He was a friendly fellow, according to Wyllys McElroy who used to deliver newspapers to him. **THE HERMIT**

Another man who has fond memories of bygone days at Minnehaha Creek is Gene Ford, now of southern Minnesota. Gene remembers going over to Fifty-third and York Avenue South with his dad. His dad had his horse and scraper along and smoothed out the yard of a white, colonial cottage-type house that his friend, Arthur Bogren, an architect for the Keith Corporation, had just built on the east side of the street near the creek. From there, ten-year-old Gene and three other boys followed Minnehaha over to the Upton creek bridge (wooden at the time) and caught clams and put them in rows across the creek. The clams were up to three inches in size. He wrote, "I think we had 150!!" The year was 1928.

Ford at one time lived at Fifty-third and Queen "below the street level, toward the creek," and he once lived at Fifty-fifth and Washburn and several other places near the creek. He remembers helping his dad cut hay at the site of the present Mount Olivet Lutheran Church by the creek on Knox Avenue South. There used to be tennis courts between the site of the church and the creek.

A boy, who grew up to become fire chief of Edina, lived across the street from us. He is now retired. It was his dog, Spike, that came over to our house from a house across the alley; and Spike barked by our back door until mother followed the dog to where my little sister was hanging, helplessly, upside-down, with her foot caught between the branches of a tree.

After or during a rain, when there was no thunder or lightning, we children liked to run barefoot in the puddles along the gravel road. The cool water and muddy sand seeping between our toes was a balm to our feet. Wading in Minnehaha felt the same way—only better—because of the soft, deep sand. Of course, after a lengthy or heavy rain, Minnehaha Creek would run fast for a few days, rejuvenated by the downpour.

During the drought and heat of the Depression, we slept with small fans on all night, or else we slept in the basement. There was no amusement room down there, but it was cool, comfortable and clean, in spite of a coal bin in one corner. Another method of cool-

ing off, for kids, was running in water sprayed by the lawn sprinkler.

Two radio shows the neighborhood kids enjoyed were Fibber *McGee and Molly* and *Tarzan*. Sometimes boys and girls grouped around the radio like a T.V. audience of today. Fibber McGee had an overflowing closet, and many a packed closet today is known as Fibber's closet. As for Tarzan, we thrilled to Tarzan and Jane adventures. This led to attempts to copy Tarzan's vine and tree-swinging feats when we were at the creek. On one occasion, the smallest one of us swung last and broke a branch and her ribs. Suppressing laughter, we helped her home.

A quiet summer activity for creekside kids was the creative craft of filling glass jars with layers of colored sand. We used white sand from a sandbox, usually, and dyed it with berry juice or food colors. Ada Mayhew Dorn (who grew up at Pleasant Avenue and the creek) says that kids from all over used to dig into the varicolored layers of natural sand in the river banks and caves at the mouth of Minnehaha Creek to get sand for their sand-bottle hobby. The method used was to put different-colored sand in piles around the inside of a jar, using a teaspoon—then pack the sand in tight—and cap it. The design could last for years. Useless as the sand bottles were, except for decoration, making them was a creative hobby that children—and some adults—enjoyed.

ADA MAYHEW DORN

The sand creations even became a small business. Theodore Wirth noted in his *Minneapolis Park System* book that the Park Board granted the privilege of erecting a booth and selling sand novelties in 1919 and later, to Edith Fischer.

Fourth of July celebrations in our neighborhood were exciting times. One place we bought fireworks was on France Avenue South at Forty-fourth Street where a big awning of striped bunting, in flag colors, was put on the front of a store. A charitable organization sold fireworks there; and we could pick and choose from the many varied and colorful firecrackers, fountains and rockets. The huge red, white and blue display caused us to debate about our selections almost as much as for candy at the crick store.

We bought ladyfinger firecrackers, cherry bombs and throw-type torpedos which exploded when thrown against the sidewalk. Although our dad thought he had put the fireworks out of reach of the children, one year my tomboy sister sneaked out early, without supervision, and exploded a cherry bomb beside her toe because the bomb was a dud and exploded unexpectedly when she was off guard. She had to sit with her foot in a bathtub of cold water most of the day.

FIRECRACKERS

A harmless novelty, which we sometimes had on the Fourth, was a little shell that opened into a pink or red lotus flower, or an American flag, when the shell was dropped in water. A glamorous neighbor girl, who visited the Taj Mahal on her honeymoon in India, brought some of the magic lotus flowers back for us, and we thought they were exotic. Certain

Minneapolis variety stores had the flags. They may become available again. An Afton, Minnesota toy store got some of both the lotus and flag shells in the summer of 1989; but they had to be sent back to the supplier—they would not open.

We used a tan stick of smoldering punk to light loud, two-inch firecrackers. Their long fuses would sizzle when lit and sometimes fizzle out. Gray pills, about one-half inch across, turned into curling, black-ash snakes up to a foot long after they were lit with a match.

After dark we enjoyed amazing one and two-foot sparklers which, when ignited, metamorphosed into hissing, sparkling fairy wands that allowed us to command our personal kingdoms for a minute or two. When a sparkler burned out, we were left with a hot, ugly, bent wire.

We four sisters were used to gunpowder and the noisy report of guns because our dad was a gun hobbiest and was active in local gun clubs. A former soldier and military policeman in World War I, he often took us on hikes along Minnehaha Creek before there were very many houses there. We sometimes shot at cans or small targets in that pastoral setting—with bees humming in the white and purple clover—daisies, columbines and violets peeking out of the grass—and the murmur of creek waters rippling through the green valley.

On a few occasions during the Depression years, dad took his shotgun over to the cornfields on farms south of York Avenue and the creek and shot a pheasant for supper. Rabbits, squirrels, ducks and deer were also the meat for supper on rare occasions. We four girls, however, preferred the meat course to be from Ben Grossman's little grocery store on Fiftieth and Xerxes Avenue South. This grocer helped select groceries and would charge and deliver them; and a butcher would prepare meat to order in his little shop in the back of Ben's store where the butcher shop floor was covered with fresh sawdust each day.

EDDIE
BLUMBERG
AND THE
AUTHOR
ON A "TRIKE"
1926

WINTER

One winter, around 1931, Minnehaha Creek froze as smooth as a mirror. There was no snow cover, and we could skate from Fifty-fourth and Xerxes for blocks either way on the winding creek. A particular, memorable day that winter, the weather was mild enough so that we could skate for hours. Our resting spot was a quaint, wooden foot bridge which crossed the creek at about Chowen Avenue South. We made sure we wore wool socks. There was no warming house.

Other winters it looked like the creek froze as it rippled because there were rough overlappings of ice. Skating then took more skill. On rare occasions someone's foot went through the ice, but no limbs were frozen as we hurried home to dry out. We didn't know anything about "wind-chill factor" and that our faces could freeze in certain temperature and wind conditions. Our skin must have been conditioned to the cold from walking to and from Robert Fulton grade school, two round-trips a day. It was required that we go home for lunch except for one or two days a year in extremely bad winter weather. It was exciting and fun to eat our bag lunch at school when it was allowed. The poor teachers often ate food prepared by the cooking class, such as gingerbread without the ginger. There was no school lunch program.

SKATING 1928
You were expected to grow into your skates.

Real horsepower cleared the sidewalks and alleys during the 1920s when men with horses were hired to help plow passageways through the snow after a big snowstorm. Most used a team and a V-shaped plow.

Older girls in the 1920s did not wear leggings — and certainly not slacks as they were not popular then. Leggings were only for little girls and boys—except for ex-soldiers, like our dad, who wore World War I winding-strip leggings (four inches wide) of khaki, for winter sportswear. Instead of leggings, older girls wore long, white lisle stockings with wool underwear, which came to our ankles and folded over in a lump. We also wore black buckle overshoes and fairly long coats. Pants were considered mannish, but in the 1930s, we wore wool ski pants for skating and skiing and shorts and slacks for sports-wear.

WINTER CLOTHING

Our little house, with four rooms, bath and porch, had a coal furnace, which was stoked morning and night in the coldest months. All the heat came up into the house through a heavy, 4 by 4 foot iron grate near the center of the house. When we children came in covered with snow and ice, we stood over the grate and warmed up and dried our clothing.

We observed Christmas at church and school with Christmas carols and special programs. At home, we usually selected a fragrant, balsam Christmas tree that perfumed the house during the holidays. A friend told me that around 1920 big, flatbed, horse-drawn sleighs came through the neighborhoods, delivering postal packages for Christmas. There were several postmen on the sleighs, including extra help hired for the Christmas rush. Children watched and hoped that a

package or two would be delivered to their houses.

Stockings were pinned to the velour davenport with care,
with hopes that Santa would soon be there.

At our special Christmas day dinner, sometimes, we would all be sleepy because one sister would pop out of bed about three in the morning to see what Santa Claus had brought; and the folks could not get her back to bed for very long. Memorable gifts over the years were: clothing; an authentic, red fire engine; dolls; a blue Marmon roadster pedal car; skis; skates; a toboggan; sleds, trikes and bikes; and, once, a Lionel electric train. Any skating or sliding equipment was promptly used at the nearby creek.

The winter of 1939 mother and I sewed skating skirts, of midnight-blue velveteen, for my three little sisters. We also made matching bonnets, trimmed with a white furry cloth. The girls had taken a few park-sponsored skating lessons and wanted to imitate the famous Norwegian-American figure skating star, Sonja Henie. Our whole family had seen her enchanting performances in movies at the Edina Theatre, such as in her 1937 films *One in a Million* and *Thin Ice*. Christmas day, 1939, with the Edina millpond as the setting for the girls' debut, they did a few spins, bows, glides, kicks and falls, trying out their new, white, figure skates and homemade skirts and caps.

ON EDINA
MILLPOND

Author with
Little Sister,
Connie,
1939

The days right after Christmas were always a bit sad for us because it would be a whole, long year before our favorite holiday time came again.

The hills on the north banks of Minnehaha Creek from Washburn to York Avenues were probably the best sliding spots on the creek. Neighborhood children wore out their sleds, skis and toboggans along that stretch. We swooped down the hills to the creek, dipped a foot onto the frozen creek and up the other side. There were few trees. One boy supervised and built a bobsled run west of the steep cement apron which drained Washburn Avenue into the creek at Fifty-fourth. Only the most daring boys chose to zip down it on sleds or cardboard.

There was a spot on the northeast hill at Minnehaha Creek, on Fifty-fourth and Xerxes, that was a big sheet of "rubber" ice one year, and often the creek had shaky, rubber ice, with water just under the surface,

towards spring. Our gang of girls spent hours bouncing on the rubber ice, daring it to crack. It was our free trampoline.

Our house was on a route that a farmer used for sleigh rides on winter evenings. As the horses and sleigh came over the Minnehaha Creek bridge on Xerxes and turned west towards our house, we could hear the crescendo of the sleighbells and happy voices of the kids—and the driver's "gitty-up" shout to the horses—as the sleigh glided over the snowy streets.

The creek neighborhood was a great place to grow up!

Playful sketch of Creek Memories by Leone Wadsworth Howe

Chapter 8

The Lake Harriet Tributary

After the York to Penn Avenue stretch, our creek map shows portages at Logan and James Avenues. However, the City of Minneapolis is improving the bridges (1993-95) for better canoe passage and anti-flooding purposes. At Humboldt Avenue and about Fifty-first Street, a stream from Lake Harriet used to flow into Minnehaha Creek; but a road now separates the lake and the creek branch. Humboldt Avenue will also get an improved bridge.

The little branch stream bed is heavily wooded, and this woods is one end of a bird sanctuary that extends east along the main creek to Nicollet Avenue. The area provides good nesting spots. At Humboldt Avenue today, the branch stream runs by Lynnhurst Field and Park and Burroughs School. The picture below, taken near the Lynnhurst Bridge in 1908, shows Minnehaha Creek in a much more wild state than the way it appears now.

Coates P. Bull wrote about the early days on the creek tributary that came out of Lake Harriet around the turn of the century. Bull was born and raised on the James A. Bull farm of one hundred sixty acres, in the Fiftieth and France vicinity, in a home that was built where the creek came nearest to Fiftieth Street. He recalled the pickerel, bass, sunfish and suckers which deposited their eggs, or spawn, annually in the quiet sidestreams of Minnehaha. "Suckers and Redhorse each spring swam from Lake Harriet through the outlet into Minnehaha not far from" where Mount Olivet Lutheran Church is today. Bull wrote, "They 'paid toll' aplenty; for settlers, even from Eden Prairie and miles to the west, brought their spears to harvest bushels of these fish to eat and to feed pigs."

He also described the scene at shallow rapids when the three and four-pound suckers, going upstream, caused a lot of splashing. "Farmers living close to the creek could, and did, go down with forks and pitch the fish out onto the banks for their fish fry."

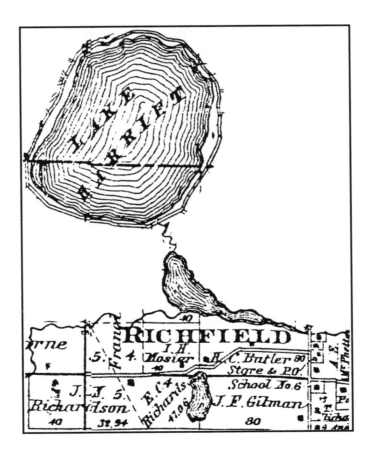

LAKE HARRIET
TRIBUTARY
1879

Walter Pardee,
Minneapolis
Architect,
wrote that
Minnehaha Creek
widened
into a swamp
south of
Lake Harriet
circa 1870.

Chapter 9

The Site Of Richfield Mills

JAMES
DUNSMOOR

Only a ghost remains of Richfield Mills, a former creek settlement at Lyndale Avenue and Minnehaha Creek. A man named James A. Dunsmoor started things in motion for a mill after he bought a claim with an unfinished house on two hundred and sixty acres for one hundred dollars in the winter of 1852-53. The claim ran from the present Fiftieth Street and Lyndale Avenue out what is now Lyndale, south for three-quarters of a mile. Minnehaha flowed through the acreage.

Soon James Dunsmoor sold twelve acres by the creek, for two hundred dollars, to a company that built a gristmill. Built in 1854, the Richfield Mills flour and feed mill used to be on the creek close to Fifty-third and Lyndale Avenue. The mill company owners were partners Philander Prescott, Eli Pettijohn and Judge Willis Moffett. The Prescott family lived on a farm near Minnehaha Falls. Prescott soon became the sole owner of the mill; but in 1860 he sold one-half interest back to Moffett. Philander Prescott remained a co-owner of the mill until his tragic death during the regional warfare of 1862. He was killed while serving temporarily at the Lower Sioux Agency on the Minnesota River. Just before the outbreak of trouble, Little Crow urged Prescott to leave. Knowing that his Sioux wife and family would be safe, he started fleeing on his Indian pony down the southern bank of the Minnesota, in the direction of Fort Ridgely. Sixty years old and heavyset, Prescott fled as fast as possible, but he was caught by two men he knew well—but who, on orders, shot and killed him. Soldiers found his body twelve miles from Fort Ridgely.

OLD
RED
MILL

The site of the old mill dam is under the present Lyndale bridge at the creek. One of only three bridges across the creek in the mid-1800s, the bridge at the Richfield Mills made what was then called Bloomington Road a direct route to Minneapolis from the countryside. The mill was commonly known as the Old Red Mill and at one time was called Richland Mills. Settlers from as far as sixty miles away came to the mill to have their grain processed, and many stayed overnight at the Dunsmoor house. James Dunsmoor became postmaster of a post office that was established near the mill.

Dunsmoor's son, Irving, who grew up on the creek at Richfield Mills, recalled that there were huge quantities of pickerel and large suckers in Minnehaha Creek when he came there in 1853. One fish trap could catch such a pile of fish that it looked like a small haystack. His family salted them and packed them in barrels for preservation. "We used to spear the fish and sometimes would get two upon our spears at once," said Dunsmoor.

In the 1860s, the Richfield Mills community had the gristmill, a school, a store, two churches and a blacksmith shop. One blacksmith, Charles Fassler, donated a picture of his shop at 5225 Lyndale Avenue South to the Hennepin County Historical Society. His building was a one-story, false front building, and wagon parts and a sled are near the building in the wintertime picture.

CHARLES FASSLER'S BLACKSMITH SHOP ON THE CREEK AT LYNDALE JANUARY 20, 1908 *Courtesy Hennepin History Museum*

John S. Mann built the first store at "Richland," which was later called Richfield. It served mill customers. Philander Prescott built the second store in Richfield when he owned the mill. Irving Dunsmoor also built a store, on an acre of his father's farm, about 1872, near the mill. He operated it a few years: then he sold it to J. N. Richardson. Sometime after the sale, almost all the Dunsmoors moved to California. One, who stayed in

JOHN S. MANN

Minneapolis, was a son, Dr. Frederick A. Dunsmoor, a physician and surgeon.

> Note: Son of James A. and Almira Mosher Dunsmoor, Dr. Frederick A. Dunsmoor was born May 28, 1853 in Richfield. Doctor Dunsmoor pushed for the establishment in 1881 of Minneapolis' first medical college, the Minnesota College Hospital, and he became its dean. In 1879 he was county physician for Hennepin County, and in 1889 he took the chair of operative and clinical surgery at the University of Minnesota. His specialty was gynecology.

BAIRD AND COMPANY

By 1881, the Richfield Mills business was operated by Baird and Company. At one period, the mill produced two barrels of flour an hour during the ten-hour working day, or twenty barrels. The waterpower was good at Richfield Mills, and the mill had four runs of stone and a turbine water wheel. It was in existence until about 1886. The success of the Richfield Mill at its beginning has been cited as a spur to the building of the Edina Mill in 1857 in what was then a western part of Richfield.

RICHLAND MILL, 1860 LATER, RICHFIELD MILLS Lyndale Avenue at Minnehaha Creek

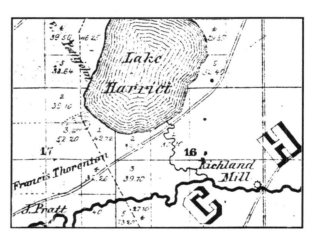

Chapter 10

Creek Memories At
Pleasant, Nicollet and Portland Avenues

For canoeists, there is another portage on the map at Grand Avenue. Ada Mayhew Dorn, who lived on Forty-sixth and Pleasant near the creek around 1917, says she swam in the creek at Pleasant Avenue almost every summer day and picnicked on a grassy spot along the stream. Neighborhood children walked around the Washburn Tower and straight down to the creek where there was a broken-down dam. They swam in the shallow waters upstream from the dam and dived in a deep pool on the downstream side. When the creek was rerouted, the swimming spot was spoiled.

PLEASANT AVENUE
GIRLS
IN MINNEHAHA,
1916

Ada Mayhew Dorn,
left center front and
her sister, back right.
They swam in *midi*
blouses and
bloomers,
using water wings.

Waters of Minnehaha passing under Nicollet Avenue at Fifty-second Street used to supply water for drinking and household uses for the Washburn Memorial Orphan Asylum home, which was built in 1886 at Fiftieth Street and Nicollet Avenue South. No record exists of how water

was obtained for the building the first six to seven years; but by 1893 water was pumped from Minnehaha Creek through a six inch main, up a hill and into a water tower—then to the Washburn orphans' home. An artesian well by the creek supplied water in the winter months. By fall, 1899, use of creek water had to be discontinued due to pollution, allegedly from refuse water of a factory upstream in St. Louis Park. The factory was struck by a tornado in 1904 and it burned down the next year.

There were several epidemics at the orphans' home, but there was no definite link to the factory or creek water. It was not until 1915 that the orphans' home finally was served by the City Water Works Department of Minneapolis. Two wells evidently served in the interim.

A few blocks beyond Nicollet on the creek, at Portland Avenue, there used to be a very popular old swimmin' hole in the 1900s. This Portland Avenue swimming hole had a diving board. Little Marlys Gervais used to swim there in 1917. She lived on Forty-eighth and Clinton. Her folks told her not to go *on* the diving board, but she went *under* it. Someone dived, and she was pushed under the water. Luckily, her father saw the accident and rescued her.

ADA MAYHEW DORN
AT A CREEKSIDE
PICNIC, 1916
The sunbonnet
buttoned so that it
could be laid flat
for ironing. Her
enamel pail was for
drinking water.

PASTORAL SCENE,
MINNEHAHA CREEK
NEAR FIFTIETH AND
NICOLLET, 1900
*Courtesy Hennepin
History Museum*
View is below the hilly
area known as
Tangle Town, also
as Washburn Park and
Washburn Hill.
Here, Creek water was
pumped through a
six-inch pipe up
to a water tower for the
Washburn Orphan's
home, 1893-1899.

Chapter 11

Lakes Nokomis And Hiawatha

About twenty-two city blocks downstream, the creek flows between Lakes Nokomis and Hiawatha. There is a portage at Nokomis and a stream from it to Minnehaha Creek. Then the creek runs through the golf course beside Lake Hiawatha and through the south end of the lake.

On old maps Lake Nokomis is shown as "Amelia Lake" and Lake Hiawatha is shown as "Rice Lake." Lake Nokomis is south of the creek and Lake Hiawatha is opposite to the north. The lake names were changed to link three important characters in Long-fellow's *Song of Hiawatha*, Hiawatha, the Indian warrior, Nokomis, his grandmother, and Minnehaha, his bride. This 1916 U.S. Geological Survey Map still shows Rice and Amelia, although the Park Board renamed Amelia in 1910. Rice Lake was renamed Hiawatha much later in 1925. Note that the creek was not connected to Nokomis at that time. Many people feel that the Indian-myth names add enrichment to the neighborhood.

1916 MAP
Note original names of lakes, Washburn Orphan Home, Lake Harriet outlet and the pool where it joins Minnehaha Creek.

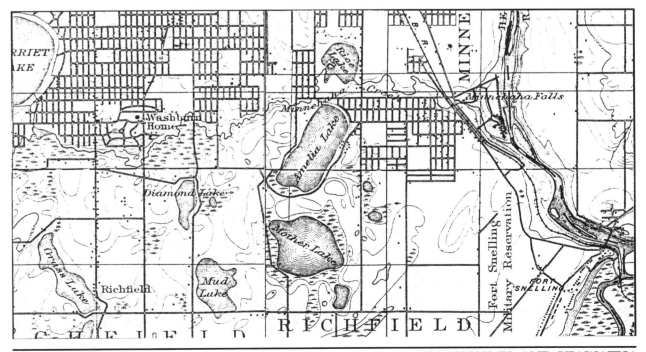

As with almost all of Minneapolis' other lakes, there was a lot of dredging, clearing, grading and fill work necessary to transform old swampy Amelia and Rice lakes into the attractive lakes, Nokomis and Hiawatha, with Minnehaha Creek running between them, and all surrounded by park land and parkway boulevards. The pioneer work of Theodore Wirth, Superintendent of Parks, 1906-35, developed the city's

lakes and streams and saved them and other open space for public use. He was recruited through the efforts of Park Commissioner Charles M. Loring and also served as Superintendent emeritus from 1935 until his death at 86 in 1949. Inspired by the work of Frederick Law Olmsted, who designed New York's Central Park, Daniel H. Burnham who designed the Columbian Exposition in Chicago and prepared plans for whole cities, including Minneapolis, and Horace W. S. Cleveland, an urban landscape architect who lectured in Minneapolis, Wirth and his associates made Minneapolis' park system the envy of many cities in the nation.

The 1921 picture, opposite, shows horses pulling the road-building equipment of the day, including hopper wagons and earth movers, with wooden-spoke wheels, scraping up the dirt. There are lots of men at work and in the foreground are the workmen's cars. Four are open-sided touring cars with leatherette tops, and one is square-roofed, with glass windows. The picture illustrates the manpower and horsepower that contributed to making the beautiful scene at Lakes Nokomis and Hiawatha and Minnehaha Creek today.

Not only decorative, Lakes Nokomis and Hiawatha offer swimming and fishing, a result of work and planning by the City of Minneapolis and its Park and Recreation Board. The Department of Natural Resources stocks Nokomis with northern pike and walleyes. The lake is well known for its sunfish and crappies.

In the back of *The Hiawatha Primer*, an 1898 school book by Florence Holbrook, there is reprinted a letter from Alice M. Longfellow, a daughter of Henry Wadsworth Longfellow, about how her father pronounced the name Hiawatha:

> *Craigie House*
> *Cambridge*
> *November 12, 1897*
>
> *Messers. Houghton, Mifflin & Co.*
>
> *Dear Sirs:*
>
> *The pronunciation used by my father was "He-awa-tha," the accent on the first syllable being slighter than on the "wa." The "a" sounded like "a" in "mar," not "war," as sometimes used. I should be glad to have this impressed on the public.*
>
> *Yours sincerely,*
> *Alice M. Longfellow*

Alas, poor Alice! I remember when the pronunciation *Heawatha* was as common as *Hiawatha* but it has pretty much disappeared now.

Florence Holbrook's book sought to teach good penmanship as well as something about Indians. These are some illustrations from her work:

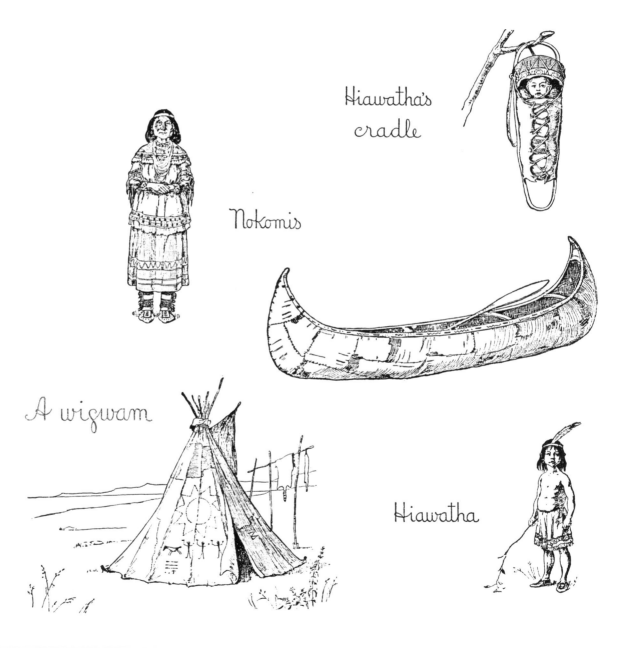

Hiawatha's cradle

Nokomis

A wigwam

Hiawatha

III
MINNEHAHA FALLS AND VICINITY

Stories About the Falls Neighborhood

Chapter 12

Longfellow Zoological Gardens
And The Zoo's Proprietor
Robert F. *Fish* Jones

Downstream from Lake Nokomis it is about fourteen city blocks to the site of a fascinating former zoo and, from there, a short walk over to Minnehaha Falls and Park. For canoeists, there is a portage at Thirty-ninth Avenue and a *Take Out* before the Forty-first Avenue railroad bridge and dam and Hiawatha and Minnehaha Avenues. After a lot of rain, the rush of water in this area could plunge one over the falls. Even with a portage around the dam and waterfall, the half mile below the falls to the mouth of the creek can be turbulent; and it is best to walk the beautiful nature trail beside Minnehaha that leads to the Mississippi River.

REPRODUCTION OF LONGFELLOW'S NEW ENGLAND HOME AT LONGFELLOW GARDENS
From *Longfellow Gardens* Jones' 1928 Pamphlet
Courtesy
Sharon Siegrist

But, first, the story of the zoo that thrived across from Minnehaha Park,

RESTORATION
IN PROGRESS

to the west, at the beginning of this century. On this property, behind the so-called Longfellow House, lived the largest and most fierce animals that were by Minnehaha Creek in recorded history.

On a visit to the zoo site in the summer of 1989, there remained only zoo proprietor Jones' recently-painted, light-yellow Longfellow House replica at the front of a big, level lot. To the rear of the lot there remained a statue of Henry Wadsworth Longfellow, with a broken nose and other ravages of time and vandalism. A pump-house that used to pump water to embellish the nearby falls was the third, and last, visible remnant of the former zoo. Minnehaha Creek flows by at the rear of the property.

Robert *Fish* Jones built his two-story, yellow, colonial home as a slightly smaller copy of Henry Wadsworth Longfellow's home in Massachusetts. The house became known as the Longfellow House. Longfellow was Jones' favorite author, whose poem, *The Song of Hiawatha*, made Minnehaha Falls famous—therefore the house and Longfellow statue.

Jones and his family lived in his Minnesota version of the Longfellow House. Not only the exterior of Jones' house duplicated Longfellow's Massachusetts house, but the interior also duplicated many details. Like its eastern twin, dinner at Jones' Longfellow House was brought up from the basement on a dumbwaiter; and there was an oval mirror over the parlor fireplace and a clock on the stairs like the eastern house. There were also furniture reproductions that were placed in the same locations as in the original.

The zoo site is quiet now except when the Seabees and the Longfellow House Restoration Group are painting or repairing the house. But, looking back to 1907 and about twenty-seven years thereafter, a lot of crowd noise and music and bird and animal squawks and roars came from the zoo.

During his zoo days, 1907 to November, 1930, when he died, Robert F. Jones used to appear in parades, or go to vote, riding in a carriage drawn by Shetland ponies, with up to twenty of his Russian wolfhounds running beside the carriage. For these appearances, he wore his usual garb of a high silk hat, Prince Albert (coat) and trousers.

Jones wrote in 1928:

The Longfellow Zoological Gardens are the property of Robert F. Jones...

The sole finances are obtained by the fee system...Situated in and surrounded by City Park property and receiving favorable consideration from the Board of Park Commissioners in liberal provision for parking space and other courtesies...Manager Jones endeavors to maintain the Gardens in a sanitary manner...(like) a Municipal Institution which is his desire to live to see as the ultimate result of his labor and investment.

After passing the yellow frame Longfellow House, one arrived at the entrance to the zoo east of the house. Often eagles were chained on each side of the administration-entrance building. Inside the entrance, to the right were the aviaries. The ornamental and Oriental birds had divided yards, and next came the large flying cage where there were cranes, blue herons, mandarin, mallard and rosy bill ducks, swans, cormorants, geese and pelicans. Another section had birds of prey such as hawks, falcons, eagles and owls.

The gray granite statue of poet Henry Wadsworth Longfellow stood on LONGFELLOW a slight rise of ground in the center of the grounds. The statue was STATUE unveiled there on June 25, 1908 with ceremonies and celebrities.

Jones described the seal act in 1928:

> The sea lion rookery is at the end of the lagoon, and here there is always a crowd watching these odd amphibious creatures disporting themselves. They are naturally intelligent and the quartet has been trained to all sorts of tricks in the water and on land. They are inordinately fond of fish, and when feeding time comes they get out on the rocks and perform various antics which are ofttimes quite comical and always amusing. They are very fond of Manager R. F. Jones, who has taken great pains to train them and for him they will do all sorts of stunts. No single feature of the Gardens is more popular than the performing sea lions. Minnehaha, Pau-pu-kee-wis, Hiawatha and Nokomis are the names of the four cross-country performers which work by command like a field of well-trained hunting hounds.

One thing that must have drawn *Fish* Jones to the Minnehaha Falls and Creek neighborhood was his interest in horses and a horse racing track at Thirty-sixth Street and Minnehaha Avenue. In the 1890s, the Minnehaha Driving Park was one of the most famous horse racing tracks in the country. However, by March, 1903, the land lease for the park expired, and the buildings were torn down. R. F. Jones, secretary of the Minneapolis Driving and Riding Club, scheduled their annual race and horse show at Hamline.

Racing was Jones' favorite sport, and M.W. Savage asked him to find a racehorse for him. Jones found the pacer, Dan Patch, in 1902 at Kansas City, and Mr. Savage purchased the horse for a reported sixty thousand dollars. The gentle horse became a sensation for pacing, such as a mile in 1:55 at St. Paul in 1906.

December 1, 1906, Jones bought the land for his Longfellow House, Gardens and zoo a few blocks south of the racetrack and across the street

ENTRANCE AND ADMINISTRATION
BUILDING — AN ADDITION 100 FEET
IN LENGTH RECENTLY ADDED
From Jones' 1928 Pamphlet,
Longfellow Gardens
Courtesy Sharon Siegrist

Daily Program

Gardens open at 8:00 A. M.
and close at 10:00 P. M.

FREE EXHIBITIONS 3:00 TO 5:00
EVERY AFTERNOON

Full Military Band Concert from 2:00 to
10:00 P. M. Sundays. Good Music Every
Hour, Every Day

ARENA EXHIBITIONS EVERY
AFTERNOON AND EVENING

Free exhibitions consist of performances by the Sea Lions, "Teddy Bears"—
four fine furry fellows—"Air Ships" and
other fur and feather features every
afternoon and evening. House of Mirth
always open.

Rides on the Steam Miniature Railway
always ready.

Admission to the grounds, Adults 30
cents. Children under ten years 15 cents.
Admission to the Arena performance 15
cents.

We buy, sell, exchange and rent all
kinds of birds and animals.

and west of Minnehaha Park. People were already accustomed to coming to the locale to see exotic animals because the park board started a small zoo there in 1894. It included deer and elk in a large penned area downstream from Minnehaha Falls. By 1906, park authorities faced such problems with their zoo as somewhat cramped cages for some of the animals, sanitation difficulties, the need for park police to occasionally break up fierce fights between male elk and, the main problem, lack of adequate funds, or the desire, for a large zoo at the falls. Under the 1906 park superintendent, the zoo was dismantled.

This was an ideal situation for *Fish* Jones' new zoo where he displayed the animals he had moved from his little animal compound downtown, some birds and animals he had purchased on a 1907 trip to Europe and the Minnehaha Park animals which the park board turned over to him in May, 1907.

The zoo that Jones developed featured caged lions, bears, seals, jungle cats, elephants, camels, Tasmanian devils, and other animals and birds. Free shows, such as performing seals or flying pelicans, were given every day from three to five in the afternoon. *Fish* Jones roamed all over his zoo, striving to see that everyone had a good time and acting as barker and trainer for most of the animal acts: "See the wonders of the world. The largest menagerie of wild animals in the whole northwest. Come see! Come see!"

Admission to the grounds in 1912 was fifteen cents for adults and ten cents for children under ten. Admission was ten cents to special acts, such as Jones' ten performing white Russian wolfhounds. Camel, elephant and miniature steam railway rides were also offered to the public.

On Sundays there was a military band concert scheduled from two in the afternoon until ten at night, with good music every hour other days. Two favorite tunes were "Over the Waves" and "Stars and Stripes Forever." Jones' wife, Maud, had formerly been an opera singer, and the band often played classical songs which were dedicated to her.

When Jones had his sea lions perform, he rewarded them with fish out of a bucket, but he did not get his nickname because he fed the seals fish. He acquired the nickname because of a fresh fish market he started in 1876 in downtown Minneapolis, which market he operated for several years.

Once a roving sea lion chased a young girl and bellowed the sea lion language for "attack." The poor girl ran and screamed, but people laughed instead of helping. Finally, the girl got inside a building. Lillian M. King, mother of the author, told this story about herself.

At the front of the zoo, beautiful Shadow Lagoon was amid shrubs, vines, flowers and colorful foliage. The lagoon appeared to be a channel dug from Minnehaha Creek. Here Jones noted that there were huge

TIGER FOUNTAIN
AND ARENA

*Courtesy
Sharon Siegrist*

LONGFELLOW
LIMITED
EXCURSION TRAIN

*Courtesy
Sharon Siegrist*

"Canadian geese, the gray African sort, with white-fronted geese and the Egyptians. There are great blue herons, storks, sandhill and other cranes...and the brilliant flamingos."

A pavilion stood on a rise in the center of the grounds. It was rustic and built of oak logs. With a fine view of the grounds, it was a favorite rest spot for tired visitors.

Some of the other animals at Longfellow Gardens were elephants, anteaters and orangutans, and a pygmy hippopotamus. By the entrance building, there were cages for small animals such as varieties of squirrels, prairie dogs, mink, Guinea pigs, Coatimundi Armadillo, sloth bears, opossums, and exotic birds such as parrots, macaws and cockatoos. In a large, circular cage, with many compartments, were Wanderoo, Military, Calitrix, Rhesus and Ringtail monkeys; black and red-faced apes; Mandril and Chacma baboons and a large orangutan.

Near the miniature steam railway system were cages with bear cubs, coyotes, coons and foxes. Beyond the ape and monkey cages were pens with "big Northern black bear and our native Cinnamon, Alaskan Kodiak and other young and old," wrote Jones. Next came the rabbit hutch with many kinds and colors of rabbit. Polar bears from Norway entertained by plunging in the water, and smaller animals listed were beaver, pure white coyotes and a white timber wolf—plus badgers, porcupines, a lynx, skunk, bobcat and a rare large pair of mountain lions.

The large Arena Building, towards the back, by Minnehaha creek, was

LIONS AND LION TAMER
Exhibitions every afternoon and evening in the arena.
From:*The Story of Longfellow Gardens,* 1912.

THE PONY RING
OR "CAROUSEL"
1911 Postcard

300 by 150 feet and it housed the main animal show where trained animals of many kinds did their tricks. There was a local story about one of the lion tamers. It was recalled by Ruth Bock in her story, *Tales About "Mr. Tails"*:

> There was an arena in the zoo where cages were around the ring. They would put wild animals through their acts and even had one lion tamer who would place his head in the lion's mouth. We had heard that the trainer before (before the current one) had shaved and cut his face before his act. He placed his head in the lion's mouth—no head! This was never verified, but it gave us kids plenty to talk about.

Seating capacity for the audience in the Arena Building amphitheater was for one thousand. At the east end of the arena twenty lions had their lair. Also housed in the Arena Building were Bengal and Sumatra tigers, leopards, jaguars and pumas. The building extended out from its circular center, and outer cages contained eagles, vultures, buzzards, owls, hawks, Java and colored peacocks and, in an ostrich yard, large ostriches. Jones listed other occupants of the zoo as "prairie and timber wolves, gray and red foxes, agoutis, porcupines, opossums, raccoons, lynx, ground hogs, peccary...Around the amphitheater are quarters for the grazing animals—red, axis, sika and fallow deer, antelope, moose with their fawns, goats, camels, sacred cows, buffalo...kangaroos."

The pony ring, while not a part of Longfellow Gardens, is somewhat associated with it as it was nearby and the ponies were wintered in the

SKATING AT
HORSESHOE BEND
by Longfellow Gardens
1920

gardens while the gardens existed. The ring was at Minnehaha Falls as early as 1893, when the Park Board granted the concession to J. R. Hartzell, and as late as the 1940s. The ponies were walked in a circle. For a small fee, children could ride on a pony or ride in a wicker, so-called governess cart, pulled by a pony. Teenage boys often led the ponies. Mr. Hartzell, as the original proprietor, brought the pony stock over from the Shetland Isles in 1891. They were 34 to 44 inches in height, and they were strong and gentle.

After Jones died in 1930 at age seventy-nine, his daughter ran Longfellow Gardens until 1934, at which time the daughter and other heirs found that they legally had to give up the house and grounds to the City and Park Board because of an agreement Jones had made in exchange for permission to operate the zoo until 1934. The zoo buildings were torn down. From 1937-68 the ten-room Longfellow House served as a charming Minneapolis public library. When the library moved out, it was a ghost house for a charitable group at Halloween; but a fire and black paint damaged walls. Also, the fact that the house had no permanent occupants over the years accelerated its deterioration.

However, from a current view, the house has been restored on the outside by the Longfellow House Restoration Group, with permission of the Minneapolis Park Board. It appears, in January, 1994, that the group has succeeded in their objective of preserving the house, thanks to an overall Minnehaha Park plan by the Minneapolis Park and Recreation Board.

The rescue further involved moving it nearby, east of Hiawatha Avenue. It was rotated so that its front faces the falls area to the east and its back faces the restored Longfellow Gardens to the west. Current planning puts Hiawatha Avenue in a tunnel under the park. An architectual firm, skilled in historic restoration, was hired in late 1993 to renovate the house in cooperation with the Park Board.

"The Longfellow House will be used as a cultural, environmental and tourist interpretive center" and will be a "focal point of the park," according to the Longfellow House Restoration Group. The house today is on the National Registry of Historic Places because it is part of Minnehaha State Park, which bears the same designation.

Chapter 13

The Wickenburgs and Minnehaha Falls

Before and after the turn of the century, the Gustaf Wickenburgs lived in a house across the street from where the Jones, or Longfellow house was built, 1906-08. Gustaf worked as a caretaker in 1895 at Minnehaha Park nearby, and, among other duties, he planted trees, shrubs and flowers at the park. One of his sons, *Henry Longfellow* Wickenburg, was born in the Minnehaha Falls police house when his mother was visiting his father. Appropriately, in later years, Henry Wickenburg became a Minneapolis policeman, serving thirty-one years and retiring in October, 1958. Henry's godmother was the poet, Emily Ross Peary, who published a little poetry booklet, *Minnehaha Laughing Water*, in 1889.

The Wickenburg house was near the creek and within a short walk to Minnehaha Falls, which caused another family name decision. They named one of their daughters *Minnie* Marie Wickenburg. Her mother told her the tale that she, Minnie, came floating down the creek in a basket, and they found her; so her name was derived from the word "Minnehaha."

NOTES ON THE MINNEHAHA TOURIST CAMP
FROM MATERIAL SAVED BY MRS. KATIE EDMUNDS,
A WICKENBURG RELATIVE

Started in 1921, the tourist camp at Minnehaha Park overlooked the Mississippi and was on fifteen wooded acres. It was on land north of the Minnesota's Soldier's Home. The camp opened May First and closed about the middle of October.

In his book, *Minneapolis Park System, 1883-1944*, former park superintendent Theodore Wirth wrote, "The camp was located in Minnehaha Park because the historic spot was and always will be visited by more tourists coming from out-of-town than any other recreation area of the city." Wirth added that the tourist camp attracted hordes of tourists from all over the United States, and from Canada and foreign countries.

The big rush of campers came in mid and late June when school was out. The first four years, there was no charge for camping, but in 1925 the Park Board decided to charge fifty cents per car per night, with a ten-dollar

monthly rate.

Eight log cabins were constructed in 1927, and each contained two double beds. In July and August the camp was crowded, with a yearly average in the 1930s of ten to twelve thousand cars registered and about twenty thousand people using the camp. Twenty-five cabins were on the site by 1930, and the

MINNEHAHA
AUTO
TOURIST CAMP
Closed in 1955, the site is now the Wabun picnic area. *Courtesy Minneapolis Park and Recreation Board*

Works Progress Administration (WPA) helped construct ten more in 1936. In 1930, a peak year, the camp took in ten thousand dollars in camp space and cabin rent fees.

Around 1930, electricity use cost ten cents per day, which could provide radio, ironing and lights. Enlarged restroom facilities, hot and cold showers, and kitchen and laundry facilities were provided, all included in the fifty cent per car camping fee. There was also a cozy log cabin community house for all.

Steffen H. Jensen, the tourist camp director for at least twelve years circa 1932, felt the camp was an important feature of the city. He commented:

> Some years ago, the tourists that used the camp were often tin-can tourists, as the name goes. Probably campers got a bad name from these. [By "tin-can tourists," he meant hoboes, or transients, who heated canned food over a bonfire.] But that has all been changed. The campers now represent a high class of citizens, who camp out because they enjoy doing so, not because they are forced to do so by circumstances. The people who come here from the east, and elsewhere, invariably use Minneapolis as an outfitting place before going north. They bring thousands of dollars into the city as the result of their stay here.

There was a gradual falling off of tent use by the campers and an increase in camp trailers and camp cars. Director Jensen thought this pointed to "a general acceptance of this idea and manner of living in the world of the out-of-doors. Some of these house cars are palatial affairs, with every possible convenience, and ranging to many thousands of dollars in price." He also said the trailers were good for living off the ground and simple to use. He felt that, as in England, the house car was "being accepted more and more freely, and it is possible that the future will see a vast increase in such remarkable homes on wheels. They are a practical demonstration of how little room is really needed for a home, and where every possible square inch of space is utilized for some certain need."

The tourist camp closed during World War II due to war priorities and gas rationing. It reopened but was closed in 1955. The area is now called the Wabun picnic area.

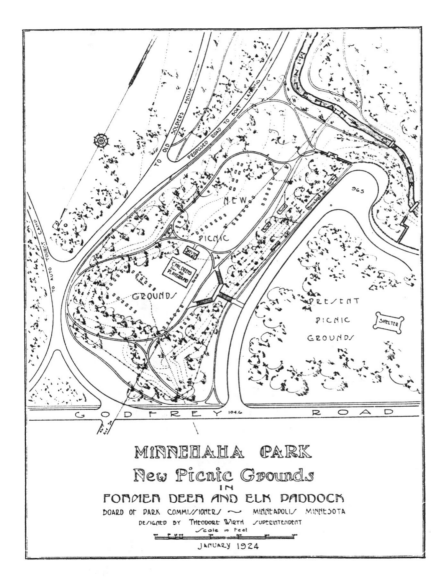

MINNEHAHA PARK
1924
Map looks southeast from Godfrey Road (now Godfrey Parkway). The road to the Auto Tourist Camp is on the far left.

Chapter 14

Minnehaha Falls and Park

Minnehaha Creek winds behind the site of the former zoo and, within a block, it becomes a slanting rapids just before it plunges fifty-three feet at beautiful Minnehaha Falls. This spot is the *creme de la creme* of the creek and has been a *must-see* spot of Minnesota for years. Usually there is at least some water coming over the falls, and after a substantial rainstorm, crowds turn out to see the cascade.

For example, one large turnout of people came to see Minnehaha Falls the first week of June, 1942. The seven pumps at, or adjacent to, Lake Minnetonka had been turned off in spring, 1942, when lake waters were just a foot below the top of the dam at Grays Bay. By the first week of June, lake waters, supplemented by rain, were going over the dam at Minnetonka and flowing to the falls. It was wartime. The local newspaper reported

PRESIDENT JOHNSON
GOVERNOR ROLVAAG
SENATOR HUMPHREY
MAKE A TWO-MINUTE
STOP TO VIEW
THE FALLS
Courtesy
Star Tribune

MINNEHAHA CREEK
110

civilian morale was stepped up by the "resurgence of Minnehaha Falls." In the week preceding June 5, 1942, an estimated forty thousand people had gone to the park to see Minnehaha Falls "Minneapolis' greatest scenic asset," according to the *Minneapolis Star Journal* at that time.

Every good rain brings people to the falls; but the Sunday after the July 23, 1987, superstorm, or "two-hundred-year" storm, people were three deep on the viewing sidewalks, bridges and platforms. Eight inches of rain poured down in five hours, with a total over two days of up to fourteen inches in some places. The flooding which resulted restored the falls to an exciting waterpower show; and photographers vied for a good spot to snap the narrow, roaring falls, which sent its spray into the crowds.

Most people would agree that Minnehaha Falls is Minnesota's most famous natural spot. Hundreds of notable people, including President Lyndon Johnson, writer Mark Twain, composer Antonin Dvorak and artist George Catlin, have visited Minnehaha Falls. The Crown Prince of Sweden and party came in July, 1926, and a news photo showed them in front of the statue of Gunnar Wennerberg, Swedish poet, scholar and statesman. The statue is the work of sculptor Carl Eldh, and it is on the south side of the creek at Minnehaha Park. Others who have admired the falls include government officials, poets, writers, composers, photographers, picnickers and tourists.

President Johnson came June 28, 1964, to address the Svenskarnas Dag (Swedish Day) picnic at Minnehaha Park. As there was only a trickle flowing over the falls that June, the Minneapolis Park Board voted to open fire hydrants into Minnehaha Creek for six hours during the president's visit. Thus, the flow over the falls was increased at a cost of six hundred dollars. SVENSKARNAS DAG

The clinching argument to increase the flow of the falls for President Johnson came from Park Board member Stefan M. Romanowski, who said:

> If you can't turn on the water over the falls for at least ten hours, then you should cut out all the post cards which show a picture of the falls. People all over the world don't know about Minneapolis, but they do know about Minnehaha Falls.

Naturalist Henry David Thoreau came from Concord to Minnesota the first two weeks in June, 1861. His doctor had advised a change of climate for his cough and lung trouble. He carried his usual equipment, such as his magnifying glass, measuring tape, note paper and a botany book. THOREAU

Near Minnehaha Falls, Thoreau saw a rose-breasted grosbeak eating slippery elm seeds; and by Lake Harriet he found that geraniums and meadow parsnips were abundant. He saw a wild pigeon's nest and several bird varieties, plus gophers, rattlesnakes and a wild crabapple tree on the prairies of Minneapolis. One of his notations read: "High blackberry most important fruit here." Unfortunately, Thoreau died in 1862, the year after his Minnesota trip.

In the *Gopher Historian* of 1965, writer Alan H. Potter called Minnehaha Falls "Minnesota's Most Famous Spot" and described it, in part:

> The historic spot in Minnesota which is best known beyond the borders of the state...as popular an attraction today as it was when settlement began in the area about 1820...the most widely honored and loved name in Minnesota history and legend.

Although Minnehaha Park had not yet been purchased by the Minneapolis Park board, one visitor to the falls, Esther P. Clark, wrote about her family's visit to Minnehaha Falls in her diary for May 20, 1879:

> John, Ella, Leon, Claudia, Fanny and myself went down to Minnehaha this afternoon to see the falls...When we reached the hotel, the hostler came out and led our horses off to the stables...and we walked through the beautiful grounds to the falls...Fanny went under the falls...picking her way carefully, but stopped several times to admire the beautiful bridal veil, as the sparkling waters are called...I found the walk nearly two yards wide, but it was very muddy and slippery most of the way...I seated myself on the bench that is placed behind the falls for the accommodations of visitors and looked through the beautiful sheet of water. It seemed very much like looking through lace curtains and as if the curtains were dotted with glass beads that sparkled and glittered in the bright sunlight.

Esther Clark is pictured in the Edina chapter of this book. In another diary entry Mrs. Clark gave a valuable description of the future Minnehaha Park:

CLARK DIARY

October 25, 1879
Mrs. Morse has been out to Stillwater for a few days but is here now and we have been to Minnehaha today to see the beautiful falls. We took the street car from Abbie's, rode down to the Nicollet [i.e., The Nicollet House at Washington and Hennepin Avenues. It was opened May 20, 1858 and built of locally made, cream-colored brick.], from there had a pleasant walk down to Washington Ave. depot and were soon on board the cars that were well filled with nice looking people. Some were going to Minnehaha as we were, and others to Chicago and distant places in the east.

Our ride was soon over and we were soon in the hotel parlors and we were glad to sit down by the good warm fire. We found there was no one in the room, so we had a good time to ourselves. We stayed here a short time viewing and making remarks about the furnishings of the room, which were very good, but somewhat worn. A waiter came to the door to inquire if we wished anything. Abbie said no, unless we would order dinner, and we had not made up our minds yet, but would let him know in time to prepare it if we concluded to stay. Abbie wanted to order the dinner, but Mrs. Morse and I did not, for I had brought my lunch and Abbie had some cake and we thought that would do until we got home.

After we had rested and enjoyed the warm fire, we went into the office and registered our names in a very large book that seemed to be full of names of people from all over the world. From here we went out through the beautiful grounds to see Minnehaha. You do not see the little beauty til you are on the brink of the cliff, for there is a cluster of trees on this side of the falls that hides from view the sparkling water of the little river where it takes this great leap to the rocky bed below. I have never seen it so low before, but it looked very pretty as it sparkled in the sunlight and all the visitors thought it a perfect little gem.

After we had had a good view from the high ground, we went around to the long flight of stairs that carries you down part way to the bed of the stream. There is [sic] over sixty steps so it is quite an undertaking, but everyone goes and feels well repaid for their trouble. The stream winds around the foot of the high hills and a narrow path is a little way up from the water. Round this path we went until we came to a mill pond. Here was an old mill on the opposite side of the river and an old dilapidated house. Tis a very lonesome place here between two high hills and I don't know who could bear to live here, but someone has in days gone by.

[Note: The buildings Mrs. Clark saw in the creek valley, near the mouth of Minnehaha Creek, would have been the first house the Godfrey family had on the creek and their gristmill, as their sawmill burned in 1867. In Chapter 16 herein, a Hennepin History Museum picture shows the old Godfrey mill she saw; and a notation on the picture says the mill was destroyed by fire on October 26, 1879, the day after Esther Clark saw it.]

Mrs. Morse gathered some shells, moss, and a few of the prettiest stones she could find to take home with her to LaCrosse. From this place there seemed no good path, and we could not climb the high hills which we wished to very much, so we turned back. We met several parties going over the walk we had been and all seemed pleased and looking eagerly for some treasure to take away with them. When we arrived at the foot of the stairs, Abbie and I went round over a little foot bridge to walk on the other side that led round under the falls. She was almost afraid to go round, but finally took courage and came round and met us on a large platform that is built out half-way up the banks. Seats are placed round for the accommodation of visitors where they can have a good view of the falls. Tall trees on the bank hang drooping over and form a cooling shade. We take our lunch at this delightful place and watched the other visitors pass back and forth behind the laughing waters. All seemed so pleased when they had been round and back, and said it was not half so dangerous as it appeared to be.

After our lunch was over we went up on the high level grounds to the hotel, and from there to Booth's beautiful gardens which are bordered with beautiful flowers but the frost had come and spoiled the beauty of most of them. There were several rustic arbors with tables and seats where in summer days it would be delightful to sit and see this grand display of flowers. The greenhouse was filled with rare and brilliant plants and Abbie and Mrs. Morse could hardly tear themselves away they think so much of flowers, but it was train time and we must go or be left. So we bid these lovely gardens good-bye and went to the little depot that is opposite the hotel [the Minnehaha Depot, which is still there in 1994].

Several ladies that had been to the falls and gardens were with us there waiting. One lady said she was here attending the Universalists Convention and was staying at some hotel where between meals she felt as if she would faint for want of food. She thought it was the Minnesota air that made her so hungry. I never saw one look so pale and tired, so I offered her the remains of my lunch—she accepted very gladly. She soon was better and said now she could wait two or three hours for her dinner, she felt so much better.

Soon we heard the shrill whistle and saw far down the track dark clouds of smoke that told us to be ready and in a few minutes we were on board and hurrying back to town. We walked from the depot up to the Nicollet. This was opening day with a number of milliners. So we called along and saw a great many elegant and costly articles. The loveliest bonnets and rich laces and bright hued flowers. Every room we went into was arranged and decorated with great taste and beauty.

After our eyes were tired of seeing so many gay and pretty things, we went into a book store and saw a great number of stereographic views, and by this time started for home. We went to the Clark House and waited for a car. The first that came along had a balky horse, so we were obliged to wait for a second. When it came along we hurried on board and was [sic] soon home.

[Note: Also in 1879, Esther Clark and her husband, John, and son, Luther, attended the Minneapolis Industrial Exposition where there was a working model of Minnehaha Falls. The roaring water of the model successfully imitated the real falls. Many other displays were in the large Minneapolis Exposition Building, including beautiful carriages and an art gallery section.]

The foregoing diary excerpts are from Esther Clark's writings which were saved by her granddaughter in Missouri and passed on to Mrs. Clark's great-great-granddaughter, Claudia Schuman, of the Twin Cities area.

MAYOR BRACKETT George A. Brackett, mayor of Minneapolis in 1873, contributed much to the foundation of Minneapolis' outstanding park system. Probably his most important work for the parks was in raising $100,000 to secure Minnehaha Park lands for the City just when the land was about to be lost forever. The Minnesota Legislature voted to establish a state park at Minnehaha Falls on March 9, 1885, but did not fund the purchase. When the funds were finally available, Minnehaha State Park, technically, became Minnesota's first state park, although it is managed by the Minneapolis Park and Recreation Board.

After the Minneapolis Park Board purchase in 1889 of one hundred twenty acres for Minnehaha Park, at a cost of $92,500, the Park Department constructed roads, bridges, toilets and a refectory building, among other improvements. In 1896 the historic John H. Stevens house was towed to the park by ten thousand Minneapolis school children, assisted by horses. Another addition was the artistic, life-size bronze sculpture of Hiawatha and Minnehaha which was placed in the creek above the falls.

ZOO A zoo at Minnehaha Park began in 1894 with a deer and elk paddock, bears, caged birds and a buffalo. More animals were added in June, 1899, when a stranded showman sold his menagerie of wild animals (such as alligators, seals, foxes and cats) to the park authorities for three hundred dollars. In October, 1899, a pit for bears was built at a cost of three thousand dollars; and in June, 1900 the park board bought twenty-five prairie dogs for the park. In a few years the problem of lack of space and proper sanitary conditions for all the animals became apparent, and some of the zoo occupants were moved to barns at Lyndale Farmstead, Thirty-ninth Street and Bryant Avenue South.

When Theodore Wirth became park board superintendent in 1906, he and his board succeeded in getting the inadequate and under-funded zoo at Minnehaha Park dismantled. Of course, this turned out to be perfect timing for the opening of *Fish* Jones' Longfellow Zoological Gardens in 1907, west of Minnehaha Park. Jones took most of the park animals over to his zoo, but deer and elk and one bear all remained at Minnehaha Park until 1923.

For several years after the Park Board purchase and creation of Minnehaha Park, conflicts arose about noisy eating and drinking hangouts at the approach to the park. Adding to the din, in 1902 there was an amusement park with a huge ferris wheel, carnival attractions and a new merry-go-round which was installed near Forty-ninth and Hiawatha Avenue. The calliope on the merry-go-round destroyed the Sunday quiet, neighbors complained. The loud music and the clouds of black smoke from the carousel's engine angered many in the neighborhood. There were efforts in the community to get rid of the entertainment place, which also featured dances

SHOO!

The superintendent of parks has informed the park board that the zoo at Minnehaha is out of place.

which were held five times a week. Despite complaints, wooden shacks for the various entertainment businesses lined the entrance to the park. A fence put up to squeeze them out was soon torn down. Combined efforts of the neighbors, newspapers, police and Minneapolis and its Park Board succeeded in getting condemnation proceedings. By May 5, 1907 the carnival area was clear and quiet and ready for landscaping into more

CARTOON
Minneapolis Tribune,
1906
*Courtesy
Star Tribune*

park land.

Walter Stone Pardee, a Minneapolis architect, wrote in his 1922 autobiography that he had seen the falls area when it was more commercial than natural; and, sometimes, in the evening shadows, the area became a rowdies' den. He visited again when the businesses had been cleared and wrote: "But this twenty-first of August, 1921, behold a wonder. There was not a store, a shop, a shanty or a stand on the grounds...At one big place is a public building, well controlled, that is used for a few stands and general public accommodation."

Pardee wrote about the creek and falls: "I am well satisfied to know that Hiawatha's Laughing Water is freed from the danger that threatened it...The flow in a brook, like the flames in a fireplace, never exactly repeats itself; and that is one of its charms. I would that for the rest of life I could live by a brook."

Park keeper Alfred Geiger used to take his son, Harold, along with him on his Minnehaha Park duties in the 1909

MRS. MARY BLACKWOOD BUEGHLY BY MINNEHAHA FALLS, WINTER, 1913
Her son used to swim by the island in the creek below the St. Albans Mill site, *circa* 1924.
Courtesy Roger Bueghly

WATER FLOW PROBLEMS

to 1919 period. They used bicycles. The son at age 84 said: "The water going over the falls then was about four-feet deep because of the drainage from the lowlands and swamp areas that have since been filled in. We could hear the falls about a mile away at night—it sounded just like Niagara."

As early as 1911 zookeeper Robert *Fish* Jones had a brick pump house by the creek behind his Longfellow Gardens. Pumping from the artesian well there could send 1,200 gallons per minute to increase the flow of water over the falls just downstream. But apparently pumping ground water is not an option today because of environmental concerns. Pumping well water for the falls could destroy the underground aquifers and bring harm to the environment at Minnehaha Falls.

The idea of pumping water back to the falls from the Mississippi River has appeared in the newspaper. It would have to be pumped, or flow, about one-half mile back; however, the worry about this proposal is pollution from the river. On the plus side, however, such pumping of river water over the falls would aerate and help purify it—and return water to the Mississippi purer and not diminished in quantity to any great extent. Another idea, published in 1964, was to divert water from Bassett's Creek, or from Minneapolis air conditioning waste water, to Minnehaha Falls during dry summer months to please visitors. It never happened.

The amount of water going over the falls today varies from little up to a rather narrow, turbulent, roaring cascade, but this has been happening for years. The variation in the flow of creek waters contributed to the decision to build the first government mill, in the 1820s, on the Mississippi at St. Anthony Falls instead of at the falls of Minnehaha Creek (then called the Little River). The most likely time to see a good cascade at Minnehaha Falls is in the spring, but Minnehaha Park gets a lot of use regardless of how much water is coming over the falls. There is a certain glamorous atmosphere there and challenging stairways down the cliffs of the creek gorge. Also, there is a wonderful nature path from the falls to the Mississippi River about one-half mile downstream.

Minnehaha Park will receive a $7 million renovation under a long-range master plan adopted by the Minneapolis Park and Recreation Board in January, 1990. The plan includes repairs, new equipment, trails and a proposed arboretum. The first $1 million funding request was submitted to the Minnesota Legislature January, 1990, and it was approved.

MINNEHAHA SPRING BED

LUPTON BROS. AD
From the 1874
Illustrated Historical Atlas published by A.T. Andreas

There are quite a few odes, songs and true tales about Minnehaha Falls, and eleven selections from the stories follow. The first story was uncovered years ago when a reporter was snooping around in an eastern library in 1900.

STORY NUMBER ONE

AN 1833 MEMOIR OF A FORT SNELLING DOCTOR

Details from an old newspaper article confirm that Minnehaha Falls and its surroundings were an attraction for Fort Snelling people in 1833. An army medical officer, who had recently arrived at Fort Snelling, sent a letter to his home town newspaper at Portland, Maine in June, 1833. The

MINNEHAHA FALLS
1910
*Courtesy kin of
Francis Erickson*

letter described "primeval" conditions at a beautiful falls near Fort Snelling and the Mississippi River. A school book, *The Story of Our Country*, by Ruth and Willis West, published in 1948, shows what is now Minnesota east of the Mississippi to be in Michigan Territory, and west of the river in Missouri Territory on a map dated 1830. Also, none of the peace and land treaties for this area between the U.S. Government and the Indian people had yet been signed—except the 1805 Pike agreement which acquired the Fort Snelling military reservation and a tract at the mouth of the St. Croix River.

The medical officer marveled at the scenery where, "Here, for the first time in my life, I beheld Indian villages...and their inhabitants," [changed little from their earlier life]. Then the doctor described the western prairies, with waving green, and breezes blowing fragrance from countless flowers. "There can be no scenery in the world more splendid and magnificent than that of the upper Mississippi, especially of that portion of it above Prairie du Chien," he wrote. The doctor told how their steamboat, *Warrior*, pulled up at Wabashaw's village. Chief Wabashaw was too old and weak to greet them, so he sent a strong, muscular man as his representative to welcome the party. The man in the role of the Chief's adjutant general was "bedecked with all the tinsel and finery pertaining to the full-dress of an Indian official." He rode a fine horse with a high wooden saddle and other trimmings and equipment that covered the horse. A few greeting words and sign language proved sufficient during the visit. All this gives the setting in 1833 as the doctor's steamboat came up the Mississippi to the fort and falls. The doctor wrote:

We soon came in view of Fort Snelling, situated on a high bluff, at the junction of the St. Peters [Minnesota River] with the Mississippi. My first sight of it was but a glance—for an intervening point of land concealed it as suddenly from my view. But this glance was like a talismanic shock to my heart—for there, broadly floating against the blue sky, through a vista of woods, I beheld the proud flag of my country! Imagine what feelings must have been mine, after so long a travel in these western wilds—what a throb of patriotic passion must have visited me, on beholding again the familiar, the much endeared vision, our country's banner, waving in sovereignty over a region which [was still the wild frontier].
Early on the following morning I set out in company with Lieutenant Vail to

visit the falls, whose roar I could easily hear from the barracks. On our way Mr. Vail entertained me with anecdotes...while I reciprocated by telling him the news (only three months old) from the States. The mail arrives here not oftener than once a month. Our steamboat had overtaken the canoe returning with it from Prairie du Chien, and (much to the satisfaction of the soldiers) we lifted it on board.

The doctor's letter was considered so interesting that it was published in the Portland, Maine, newspaper in 1833. One student thought there was some possibility that Henry Wadsworth Longfellow could have seen it as Portland was his home town. The *Washington Intelligencer*, 1833, also published it. Writing his letter beside St. Anthony Falls, the doctor described Brown's Falls—later Minnehaha:

> After crossing a beautiful prairie, interspersed with noble ash and oak trees and well watered by streams from the lakes north of us, we suddenly stopped at the mouth of a picturesque glen. I was conducted through it a short distance, when all at once was opened upon us one of the most beautiful and symmetrical waterfalls that can be imagined. This was the outlet of the lakes; a small stream which is here precipitated over a circular shelf of rocks, presenting a concave wall of water to the eye and falling forty-five feet into a regular basin below.
>
> After enjoying this sight for a short season, we pursued our route across the prairie, meeting occasionally groups of Indian girls gathering strawberries, sometimes accompanied by their beaux, dressed with most particular niceness.

The doctor described a Dakota courtship in the falls area, which pictured a warrior in colorful plumage who won the love of a beautiful Indian maiden—after negotiating with her father. That June, 1833, afternoon there was to be ball-play [lacrosse] by three groups. They had already played three days, for six or seven hours a day, without a winner.

Note:
   Who was this mysterious doctor who came in June, 1833 and wrote so effusively about Minnesota? Some writers of that time did not sign their work.
   The evident answer to the doctor-writer's identity is in a letter written by Dr. Nathan S. Jarvis, the Fort Snelling doctor on duty from May, 1833 to 1836. The key letter was sent by Doctor Jarvis to a relative in New York on June 18, 1833. Jarvis, himself, had arrived at the fort on the steamboat *Utillity* [sic] in May, 1833.

MINNEHAHA
WHEN
IT WAS CALLED
BROWN'S FALLS

Doubtless, an artist's conception, this drawing, by H. Johnson, is from *The United States Illustrated in Views* [ca. 1855].
The book describes the falls as having "soft and delicate beauty.... This cascade emits a volume of spray, which in the shining sun produces a beautiful iris.... In the vicinity the plants have a more luxuriant growth, and their leaves are colored with a more brilliant green than elsewhere."
Courtesy Hennepin History Museum

THE FALLS
IN WINTER, 1910
*Courtesy
Claudia Schuman*

Doctor Jarvis' letter of June 18, 1833 states that the steamboat *Warrior*, traveling up the Mississippi from New Orleans, had arrived the night before and was leaving Fort Snelling at noon. An army doctor, a Doctor Harris, arrived on the steamboat and brought Doctor Jarvis' box of medical books that he had, per orders, left in New York for later shipment. He could have used them on the "hot and filthy" steamboat to treat men dying of cholera.

Clues that completely match facts in the newspaper article herewith and pinpoint Doctor Harris as the author are: the *June, 1833 arrival* of an *army doctor* who had traveled on the *steamboat Warrior* from *the mouth of the Mississippi*.

Both doctors mention the ball games that were going on among the Dakota-Sioux men. Jarvis wrote, "Yesterday there was a ball game on the Prairie 1/2 a mile from the fort between 2 bands of Sioux Indians, 100 on a side." When the *unidentified* doctor-writer saw the games, they had been going on for three days.

All the matching facts make Doctor Harris almost certainly the author of the letter in question. Logically, the army would not have assigned more than two doctors to such a remote area as Fort Snelling in 1833—especially when, as Doctor Jarvis wrote, "This is the most healthy post in the United States."

STORY NUMBER TWO
THE LAUGHING WATERS
by Mrs. Mary Eastman
Regarding the "Little Falls" between St. Anthony Falls and Fort Snelling, Mary Eastman wrote in the introduction to her book *Dahcotah*: "The Indians call them Mine-hah-hah, or laughing waters."

Do you know where the waters laugh?
  Have you seen where they playfully fall?
Hid from the sun by the forest trees green,
  (Though its rays do pierce the vines between.)
Dancing with joy, till, night-like, a screen
  Comes down from the heavens at the whippoorwill's call.

Come with me, then, we will tread
  On a carpet of long grass and flowers.
The wild lady's slipper we'll pluck as it droops,
  We will watch the proud eagle, as from heaven she stoops,
A seat we will take by the dark, leafy nooks,
  Where a fairy might while away summer's bright hours...

And here does the tall warrior stand
  With the maiden he loves by his side!...
'Twould be well, did ye weep, waters bright!
  Soon no more to your banks will they come—
The maiden who loves, or the warrior so brave,
  The wild deer at eve, in thy waters to lave...

The above excerpt is from a fragile, old book called *THE IRIS, An Illuminated Souvenir*, edited by John S. Hart, L.L.D. and published in 1852.

STORY NUMBER THREE
THE TALENTED EASTMANS

Captain Seth Eastman is a venerated artist-historian of American Indian life that he saw in the Fort Snelling vicinity while he was stationed there in 1830-31 and again in 1841-48. Mary Eastman, his wife who was with him in the latter period, was a writer-historian who wrote poems and stories that often matched her husband's paintings. A peek at Seth Eastman's studio at Fort Snelling, in 1846, would reveal at least four hundred of his drawings of American Indian life and scenes along the Mississippi, recorded with his paintbrush, pencil or pen.

The Relationship Between Captain Seth Eastman and Doctor Charles Eastman

Seth Eastman was the grandfather of the Doctor Charles A. Eastman, who wrote *From the Deep Woods to Civilization* in 1916. Charles had the Dakota name of "Ohiyesa," or "The Winner." His lifetime was spent, as an

THE LAUGHING WATERS,
Three miles below The Falls of St. Anthony.

adult, trying to reconcile two cultures because he was raised by the Dakotas and had the white grandfather, Seth Eastman, a graduate of West Point and of New Hampshire stock. Charles was accepted by both cultures.

Charles Eastman's mother had been born on Lake Harriet's shores, an offspring of Seth Eastman and the woman he took as his wife circa 1830, the daughter of Chief Cloud Man of the Lake Calhoun village. The couple called their daughter Nancy; and she, in later years, married Many Lightnings. Nancy died shortly after giving birth to the couple's fifth child, Charles Eastman, one of Captain Eastman's grandchildren. This tie gave Seth Eastman both artistic and blood closeness to the Dakotas.

Little Charles fled to Canada in the care of his grandmother and uncle during the warfare of 1862. The family thought his father had been killed in the war. Charles enjoyed growing up in the forest, where he was trained as a warrior and hunter. When he was age fifteen, his father, Many Lightnings—also known as Jacob Eastman—showed up in the Canadian camp. The father had been converted to Christianity while he was an 1862 war captive, and he convinced Charles that the new trail was the way to go—to the father's northern Dakota Territory farm and so-called civilization. The trail led to reading and writing and, eventually, Dartmouth and Boston University for medical school.

At age thirty-two, 1890, Charles Eastman became a doctor; and he was able to serve the American Indians as doctor-lawyer-type advocate and author. In 1933, at the Chicago World's Fair, Charles Eastman won a medal of honor for being the most distinguished American Indian. The Indian Council Fire picked him over some fifty other nominees. He died at age eighty, in 1939.

An Untitled Poem About the
Laughing Waters

Dancing in the sunlight,
Rippled by the breeze
Laughing in the meadows,
Sighing in the trees;

When o'er the prairie first
The Indian trod,
And on his vision burst
This work of God,
No wonder he should claim it,
A lovely sight,
A laughing sprite,
And shouting forth, should name it,
With wrapt delight,
Minnehaha.

The above poem appears on pages 75 and 76 of *History of the County of Hennepin*, by W. H Mitchell and J. H. Stevens, 1868.

STORY NUMBER FOUR

LONGFELLOW'S HIAWATHA POEM

WHICH MADE MINNEHAHA FALLS FAMOUS

Henry Wadsworth Longfellow's poem, *The Song of Hiawatha*, made Minnesota and Minnehaha Falls famous through the United States and in literary circles of the world when it was published in 1855. Some known inspirations for the poem are Indian legends and lore recorded by explorer Henry Schoolcraft from his visit to Minnesota; the book, *Dahcotah*, by Mary Eastman; and a daguerreotype picture of Minnehaha Falls, which was made by Alexander Hesler of Chicago.

Recorded in historical archives for posterity is Hesler's story of the part his picture of Minnehaha Falls played in inspiring the Hiawatha poem. Hesler wrote that he came up the Mississippi in April, 1852, on the steamer, *Nominee*, from Galena to St. Paul. He took daguerreotypes of St. Anthony Falls and Minnehaha Falls, among other scenic spots. While at Minnehaha Falls, his party got a jug of water from a spring which flowed out of rocks at the foot of the falls on the right. An Irishman's claim shanty was nearby. Sometime later, Hesler gave copies of his pictures to George Sumner of Boston, Massachusetts, where Longfellow lived. One picture, of Minnehaha Falls, was Sumner's favorite, and Hesler wrote about it:

> Longfellow never was there and never saw the falls.
> "Do you remember the daguerreotype you gave me at Galena?" [Sumner said].
> I [Hesler] said: "Yes, perfectly."
> "Well, then, I got home, being neighbors, I showed him [Longfellow] the pictures you gave me, and he selected Minnehaha, took it out in the woods with him and from it he conceived the thought and poem of Hiawatha." [Sumner told him.]

Hesler received a copy of the lengthy Hiawatha poem-book, inscribed: "Mr. A. Hesler, with compliments of the Author, Jany., 1856."

A good example of Longfellow's references to Minnehaha and Minnehaha Falls is in the verses where Hiawatha asks the father, the ancient arrowmaker, for Minnehaha's hand in marriage and adds that the marriage could lead to peace between the Indian nations. Excerpts follow:

Excerpts from *The Song of Hiawatha* by Henry Wadsworth Longfellow:

> That this peace may last forever,
>   And our hands be clasped more closely,
> And our hearts be more united,

Give me as my wife the maiden,
Minnehaha, Laughing Water,
Loveliest of Dacotah women!

The ancient arrowmaker and Minnehaha consented to the marriage, and Hiawatha went off with his bride:

From the wigwam he departed,
Leading with him Laughing Water;
    Hand in hand they went together . . .
Heard the Falls of Minnehaha
    Calling to them from the distance,
Crying to them from afar off . . .
    Over wide and rushing rivers
In his arms he bore the maiden;
    Light he thought her as a feather
As the plume upon his head-gear . . .

The name "Mine-hah-hah", purportedly, is the Dakota Indian word for "Laughing water." The popularity of the poem really fixed the name Minnehaha Falls.

STORY NUMBER FIVE

THE LEDGE BEHIND THE FALLS

Although there has long been a stone bridge over the creek above Minnehaha Falls and a bridge across the stream below the falls, daredevils used to walk on the ledge behind the falls to the other side. This has been against park rules for quite a few years, but some visitors to the falls ignored warning signs and fences.

Frank Leslie's *Illustrated Newspaper* of 1869 described a close brush with death that photographer Charles Zimmerman had November 28, 1869. Zimmerman came to the falls from his home in St. Paul and planned to photograph winter views of the falls. That November day, the ice was thawing and there was water flowing over the falls. Zimmerman tried to cross the creek on the ledge behind the waterfall; and, as he stood looking at formations of ice and the falls, something hit him and knocked him out. He collapsed and lay there until he was nearly frozen.

An hour after the accident a Mr. Haines came along exploring among the rocks. He happened to look behind the falls, saw Zimmerman, and rescued him. Investigation proved that a large icicle, which weighed 200-300 pounds, had been loosened from the top of the passageway-ledge by the thaw, and it fell on Zimmerman, leaving him unconscious. The news account said a rescue one-half hour later would have been too late and Zimmerman would have died.

One-hundred years after the Zimmerman accident, the falls ledge was still dangerous. In an April, 1969, *Minneapolis Tribune* interview, Rudy

Hogberg, assistant director of the Minnesota Geological Survey, warned visitors not to venture behind the falls because of the "inherent danger" of being struck by falling rocks. He said a natural weathering process had loosened rock layers on the ceiling over the ledge. There was increased danger in spring and fall when water freezes and thaws in cracks between the rock layers. Park police had noticed rocks which had fallen that weighed up to several hundred pounds. Hogberg, in a letter to the Park Board, suggested close lookout points which would give "a more aesthetic experience at the falls—by feeling the mist of the falls, examining the rocks that support it and perhaps even touching the falling water." A Park Board planner-architect commented at the time, "He's absolutely right."

According to the *Tribune* article that quoted Hogberg, some major improvement projects at Minnehaha Park had to await the outcome of a dispute about making Hiawatha Avenue a four-lane highway by cutting through park land. A Solomon may have solved it. A proposed solution (1990) calls for a wide highway, at present called Hiawatha Avenue/T.H. 55, to run in "sort of" a tunnel under a rise of ground, thus joining Minnehaha Park to the former Longfellow Gardens zoo property.

AN ACCIDENT
UNDER
MINNEHAHA FALLS
Illustrated Newspaper
December 15, 1869
Courtesy Hennepin
History Museum

THE HERMIT OF MINNEHAHA FALLS

At the turn of the last century, a hermit lived by Minnehaha Falls in a vine-covered, sod shack. The hermit's name was William Herrick, and he lived in the gorge below the falls from 1891 until at least 1903. Visitors often asked him why he became a hermit, but Herrick did not answer the question until 1903 when he was about to move to the Milwaukee Soldier's Home. He wrote:

WILLIAM HERRICK
Courtesy Hennepin
History Museum

In the first place I suppose that the love of solitude, the desire for one's own company, is inherent in some men's systems, just as the desire for company is inherent in others. . . I loved the forest with its lovely grandeur, I loved the great prairie with its solemn stillness. But this was not my only reason for shunning human society. There was in my case what there has been in many like cases—a woman.

Born in New York City to parents he described as "poor but honest," he moved with his family to Wisconsin when he was age six. The next year his father died and his mother eventually remarried. They moved to Minnesota. His stepfather usually found two or three occasions a day to whip him for trivial offenses; therefore, at an early age he enlisted in the army to fight in the Civil War on the Union (Abolition) side. He tried to enlist in a Minnesota regiment, but they said he was too small to stop a bullet. He then enlisted in Wisconsin and was sent to Missouri. When he returned from service, his stepfather had died, "and I verily believe in doing so he saved me the crime of murder," he wrote.

The hermit claimed to be a nephew of Dr. Livingstone, the African explorer, and also said that his father was a stepbrother to Isaac Singer of sewing machine fame. In 1871 Herrick had the only romance of his life when he met and married a beautiful girl after a short courtship in Wisconsin. They lived happily together for two years. He made a living cutting wood; but a grasshopper plague brought poverty and a move further east. Herrick said his wife could not stand poverty, and one night when he returned home, he found she had deserted him. Too proud to follow her, he "cut loose from civilization" and became a trapper.

Eventually Herrick's health broke down from the privations of being a trapper, and he came to the Minnesota Soldiers' Home at the mouth of Minnehaha Creek in 1890. But soon, wanting more solitude, he started living alone in a shack he built by the creek between the Soldiers' Home and Minnehaha Falls. He was supported by his veteran's pension.

"It is enough for me to say that the woman I married ruined my life and sent me to wander on the face of the earth," Herrick commented. For most of the past twenty years he had been a recluse. His shack had vine-covered lattice trim and a flower garden. In spite of his claim to love solitude, the hermit visited with many who came to see the falls and often gave visitors bouquets from his garden.

By 1903 Herrick was ready to move out of Minnehaha Park. He wrote that he was grateful to two benefactors who were going to finance his move into the Milwaukee Soldiers' Home in Wisconsin, where he had enlisted.

THE FALLS, 1860
Note people on the ledge behind the falls.
Courtesy Hennepin History Museum

Hermit Herrick would have used the bridge pictured next. It was near his hut.

This rustic bridge was carved by skilled woodcarver Peter Joseph Winnen, who settled in the Lowry Hill neighborhood. He had a woodcarving shop on Fifth and Nicollet, and early Minneapolis grew around him. Later, he moved to the family homestead in the Wayzata area to care for his mother, and he established a woodcarving workshop there.

Originally an immigrant from Germany, Winnen carved this bridge below Minnehaha Falls circa 1900, and it was admired and photographed by throngs who visited the falls around the turn of the century. The bridge is memorialized in a panel of a wardrobe which Winnen carved. The wardrobe panel is on display at the Western Hennepin County Pioneer Museum, Long Lake, Minnesota. The panel shows Minnehaha Falls and the bridge.

RUSTIC BRIDGE
1905
Courtsey Margaret Bevan

Minneapolis city fathers sought out Winnen frequently to help build bridges and parks throughout the city. Also, Winnen carved pulpits, lecterns and other equipment for several Twin Cities churches. He liked to incorporate

birds and animals in his work; and a desk he carved like a lectern has an egret, leaves, an owl and songbirds on both sides.

THE FALLS INSPIRED COMPOSER ANTONIN DVORAK

Famous Czech composer Antonin Dvorak visited Minnehaha Falls September 4, 1893. On a trip to Omaha and Minneapolis from his summer residence in Spillville, Iowa, Dvorak especially wanted to see Minnehaha Falls at Minneapolis. As he gazed up from the foot of the falls, he commented, "It is so intensely beautiful that words cannot describe it." He then asked his aide, Kovarik, for paper, but his assistant had none with him; so Dvorak took his pencil and wrote notes on his starched shirt cuff. He knew the Longfellow Indian-myth poem about the falls, and his composition had an Indian theme. In the 1860s he had read a translation of Longfellow's *Song of Hiawatha* by a Bohemian writer.

Back in Spillville, Dvorak used the shirt-cuff theme in his *Sonatina for Violin and Piano, Opus 100*, second movement, known as *Indian Lament*. It was included in concerts in the eastern United States. Later, violinist and composer Fritz Kreisler performed his own arrangement of Dvorak's composition, and the sonatina became well known.

Indian Lament should not be confused with the *Indian Love Call* which was sung by Nelson Eddy and Jeanette MacDonald years ago in a movie, or with *By the Waters of Minnetonka, An Indian Love Song*, by Thurlow Lieurance. Kreisler's version of Dvorak's composition starts out in G minor, with three, and sometimes four, notes accented like the beat of an Indian drum—in the violin accompaniment. The sample below hints at the general theme of *Indian Lament*:

On the second sheet of the music (page 4), there is a beautiful section where the violin part emphasizes E flat and D notes above middle C three times, with rests between each two notes. Then the same notes trill four times and lower an octave, trilling three times, with the flat removed from the last E note. The expression is marked "dim." to reduce the tone and give a haunting echo effect of a lament, or Indian chant. Example:

Antonin Dvorak came to New York in 1892, by invitation, to become director of the National Conservancy in New York. He was already famous in Europe and had been appointed a professor at the Prague Conservatoire, also receiving honors from the English, Czechs and Austrians. A wealthy New York woman, Mrs. Jeanette Thurber, persuaded him to come to the United States by offering him a lucrative two-year contract. While in New York, he composed his most famous work, *Symphony No. 9 in E Minor, Opus 25,* subtitled *From the New World,* and published in 1893. Some of the scoring for this symphony was completed in Spillville, a Czech settlement. A Dvorak student said that Dvorak once claimed his New World symphony contained a part depicting the sobs of Minnehaha as she parted from Hiawatha. By 1901, Dvorak had left the New World and was back in Europe where he died in 1904.

TWO PRETTY VISITORS AT THE STATUE OF HIAWATHA AND MINNEHAHA
Courtesy Hennepin History Museum

STORY NUMBER EIGHT
JACOB FJELDE STATUE OF HIAWATHA AND MINNEHAHA

An August 5, 1902, copy of the *Minneapolis Journal* suggested that Jacob Fjelde's plaster-cast statue of *Hiawatha and Minnehaha* should be cast in bronze and erected in Minnehaha Park. The plaster version was paid for by a collection from Minnesota school children. It was used in front of the Minnesota building at the world's fair in Chicago in 1893. After that it was placed in the Minneapolis Public Library where many admired it.

Sculptor Fjelde's idea and hope was that the statue would be cast in bronze and put in Minnehaha Park by the falls. The *Minneapolis Journal* made the plea that some agency raise the money for a bronze cast of the statue and place it in the park—estimated cost $2,500. "It is a beautiful thing," the *Journal* article said, and those who have seen the statue realize the "beautiful sentiment which it represents. Hiawatha is supposed to be carrying Minnehaha across the stream. No sentiment appeals to the human heart

MINNEHAHA FALLS AND PARK
129

more strongly than that of love, and this is the central theme in the study." Subsequently, the statue *was* cast in bronze and placed on a little island above the falls in 1911. The realistic and life-size statue is still above the falls today. There it adds to the interest of the park and recalls to those who see it Longfellow's Indian legend, *Song of Hiawatha,* as well as the Minnesota historical aspect of moccasins that walked in the area years before.

STORY NUMBER NINE
*A CAPSULE DESCRIPTION OF
THE GEOLOGY OF MINNEHAHA
CREEK AND FALLS*

A brief geological history of Minnehaha Creek and Falls, from a 1916 U.S. Geological Survey, states that the glacially-caused River War-

SOUTH DAKOTA INDIANS AT THE FALLS IN 1929 AFTER ATTENDING THE INAUGURATION OF PRESIDENT HOOVER
Courtesy Hennepin History Museum

ren formed a waterfall in the limestone by St. Paul, and this waterfall gradually receded until it reached a junction with its tributary, now called the Mississippi. Then the falls receded into the Mississippi River. During its recession over the half mile of river above Minnehaha Creek, the falls became split by an island, and a west branch of the Mississippi flowed through the site of the former deer park at Minnehaha Park. When the ancient falls receded past the junction of Minnehaha Creek, Minnehaha Falls began, and it was about forty feet high. At the time of the 1916 U.S. Geological Survey, the waterfall had receded six hundred feet and increased in height to sixty feet. About six hundred feet downstream from the falls, the creek turns somewhat southward and flows in the ancient river channel to the Mississippi.

According to the survey mentioned, the creek falls about two hundred thirty feet from its source at Lake Minnetonka to its mouth on the Mississippi River. This descent is recorded as one hundred twenty-five feet from Minnetonka to the top of the falls. From, and including, the approximate sixty-foot drop in rapids and Minnehaha Falls, the rush of water toward the Mississippi descends about one hundred five feet; and the stretch after the falls has beautiful rapids after a heavy rain.

Minnehaha Creek has little erosion and, therefore, not much sediment. Recession of the falls is caused by crumbling of the bed of shale where it contacts the St. Peter sandstone and Platteville limestone in about the middle of the falls (as of 1916). After the shale weathers off, the top limestone layers slowly break off; and this process formed a wide overhanging shelf, with a sandstone, fairly dry walkway, where people liked to venture under the falls to cross the creek. As of 1990, the sandstone ledge has eroded away as far as being a walkway.

Geologist Frederic W. Sardeson wrote about the St. Peter sandstone in his 1916 survey:

> Gold in fine flakes is distributed through the upper part of the St. Peter sandstone to the value of five cents or less in a ton of sand. The aggregate amount of this gold may be very great, but there is not enough for profitable mining.

NEARLY DRY
July 1, 1939
Photo by Earl C. King

STORY NUMBER TEN

1976—WHEN THE BICENTENNIAL FREEDOM TRAIN WAS ON DISPLAY AT MINNEHAHA FALLS

Because Minnehaha Falls is such a well-known landmark in Minnesota, and is known throughout most of America, it was appropriate that Minnehaha State Park, the site of the falls, was chosen as the host spot for the Bicentennial American Freedom Train, which came there on the old railroad tracks the summer of 1976. The train was parked near the historic Princess, or Minnehaha, depot. People waited in long lines to see displays from the history of the United States. On one open car was a large replica of the 1753 Liberty Bell, with the inscription taken from Lev. 25:10 in the Old Testament of the Bible: "Proclaim Liberty throughout the Land unto all the Inhabitants Thereof."

MINNEHAHA
"PRINCESS"
STATION, 1985

This little Victorian railway station has gingerbread-type architecture and is painted maroon and harvest gold. On one of three stops on the first rail line out of Minneapolis, it was built in 1875 by the Minnesota Central Railway Co. For years three trains made eight round trips daily, bringing people to Minnehaha Park and Falls and Robert F. *Fish* Jones' Longfellow Gardens. The depot was a departure point for troops and a shipping point for supplies in World Wars I and II. Animals for the nearby zoo were unloaded at this station over the years.

The Milwaukee Railroad closed the station in 1963, giving it to the Minnesota Historical society in 1964. The historical society and the Minnesota Transportation Museum group restored and currently maintain and exhibit the 20 by 22 foot depot, with its twenty-eight-foot open platforms of Flinkote bricks. The station received the name of "Princess" after the Milwaukee Railroad owned it, and train crews referred to the attractive, ornate building as "The Princess." Today it is on the list of Minnesota's major historic sites.

STORY NUMBER ELEVEN
THE JOHN H. STEVENS HOUSE AND ITS RESTORATION

Twenty-nine-year-old Colonel John H. Stevens arrived in St. Anthony on April 27, 1849. He was a veteran of the Mexican War. In the fall of 1849, he began building a farmhouse on the west side of the Mississippi, about twenty feet above some rapids in the river, in what is today downtown Minneapolis. The carpenters he hired were Charles Mousseau, Captain John Tapper and the Indian-French voyageur, Pierre Bottineau. Stevens' house was the first permanent house built on the west side of the Mississippi in Minneapolis, and it was occupied on August 6, 1850 by Colonel Stevens and his wife, Frances Miller Stevens, whom he had married May 10, 1850. The next summer he raised wheat, oats and corn on forty acres behind his house.

The site of the Stevens house was, by a U. S. survey, on Fort Snelling military reservation land; but Stevens had permission from the Secretary of War to build there as long as he maintained a ferry on the Mississippi to move troops and supplies across the river to St. Anthony. His property became known as the Ferry Farm. It was located where today's Nicollet and Hennepin Avenues reach the west side of the Mississippi River.

To combat any hours of loneliness in the isolated, wilderness location of their house when they first moved there, Stevens had a library and his wife had a piano and other musical instruments. Mosquitos were a problem. There were swarms of them, especially at night. Neither netting over doors and windows nor smoke from a smudge pot did not completely solve the mosquito problem.

To stimulate growth of a town, Stevens sometimes gave away lots to those who would build. As the years went by, the City of Minneapolis grew around the Stevens house; and, eventually, the Stevens family moved to Glencoe to farm. By 1874, the Stevens house had been moved to Second Avenue south between First and Second Streets and served as a boarding house. The *St. Paul Pioneer,* in an article about the house in its boarding house status, ran an editorial that said the Stevens house "ought to be purchased by the city as a souvenir of municipal babyhood, as New Haven guards Washington's headquarters, Hartford the roots of the charter oak, and New York the Stuyvesant pear tree."

COLONEL
JOHN H. STEVENS
From the 1874
Andreas Atlas

The location of the Stevens house became a mystery after it was moved in 1881, and not even Colonel Stevens knew where it was; but a *Minneapolis Journal* reporter discovered the house on Sixteenth Avenue South between Third and Fourth Streets around 1893. Rather than campaign for public funding to save the house at a time when there was a recession, the *Journal* purchased the house in 1893. To preserve and restore the house, it was best to have it on public property, therefore, school children were invited to help tow it to Minnehaha Park on four platforms with wheels attached. May 28, 1896, a large gathering of school children and eight horses towed the house, with ropes, from its third site, the Sixteenth

Avenue site mentioned, in the Cedar-Riverside neighborhood, to Minnehaha Park where it is currently, on park land south of Minnehaha Creek and Falls.

The president of the Minneapolis Park Board in 1985 remembered the house before its restoration in the 1980s, "It had no personality," Patti Baker said, but she added, "I remember trudging through the snow to get to the house, thinking, 'Behind these walls are stories to tell,' " as reported in the *Minneapolis Star Journal* in July, 1985.

Some of the stories are in the historic architecture of the Stevens House and its value as a relic of the early days of Minneapolis. Actions and conversations took place there which helped the growth of Minneapolis and Hennepin County. Indian chiefs, such as Little Crow, Shakopee, Hole-in-the-Day and Good Road, had important meetings in the house. The home's owner was a famous pioneer—a state legislator, founder of agricultural societies and fairs, partner in the first suspension bridge project, publisher of newspapers, a University of Minnesota regent and an author of history books. He planned and named Washington Avenue, Minneapolis' first street, and laid out other streets. Stevens also wrote the bill which created Hennepin County. He is remembered as the "Father of Minneapolis."

The Stevens house was maintained, after it was moved to Minnehaha Park, by the Minneapolis Park and Recreation Board, which group was also involved when the Junior League of Minneapolis completely restored the house in the 1980s. Junior League members donated over thirty-five thousand hours to the project, and the list of money donors and community volunteers is very long.

In July, 1985, there was a gala event held at Minnehaha Park to celebrate the Stevens House restoration by the Junior League. Sponsors of the Stevensfest Family Fun Day grand opening were the 1985 Aquatennial, General Mills, Junior League and the Minneapolis Park and Recreation Board. There were speeches by officials from the sponsoring organizations and by Minneapolis Mayor Donald Fraser.

The house was officially opened by eight great-great-great-grandchildren of John H. Stevens. Scheduled were singers, storytellers, marionettes, a balloon release and cake. All age brackets enjoyed the festive event. People stood in line to tour the house and learn its history from costumed guides, exhibits and audio-visual displays. A different line led to huge ten-cent ice cream cones, courtesy of Bridgeman's ice cream company. A pop orchestra and Bluegrass band were scheduled between 3:00 and 5:30 p.m. The Aqua Jesters were on the program, and there were carriage rides and pony rides as well as quilters and square dancers. The one hundred thirty-six-year-old Stevens House was in fine shape after its restoration. This is the heading of the four-page program:

Stevensfest

Family Fun Day

Sunday, July 28, 1985 • Minnehaha Park

1985 Aquatennial • General Mills • Junior League of Minneapolis • Minneapolis Park and Recreation Board

In 1986, in accordance with policies of the Junior League of Minneapolis, the Stevens House was made a private nonprofit corporation, operated by members of the community. This corporation is separate from any Junior League activity or monetary support.

4901 Minnehaha Avenue   Minneapolis, Minnesota 55417   722-2220

John H. Stevens House
Birthplace of Minneapolis – 1850

The above letterhead of the John H. Stevens House, Inc. is very appropriate. It shows the Stevens house in the foreground, with a cityscape around it. It tells in one drawing how the Stevens House has been and is a center for community involvement. It was the birthplace of a community, Minneapolis, in the 1850s; and it was the focus of community projects to preserve it in 1896 and again in 1983.

Today the Stevens House is operated by the community, with a board of directors from the community as well as volunteers who handle programs, educational tours and special events. The house is open to the public daily in the summer and on weekends in the fall and spring by appointment. Even in winter, groups may tour the house by appointment.

Sometimes Captain John Tapper slept at the Stevens house when he was helping to build it. Mosquitos and wolves were numerous where they were building the house by the river in the future downtown Minneapolis. One sultry night in July, 1850, Captain Tapper found it impossible to sleep in the unfinished Stevens house because the mosquitos were unusually bad; "so he took his bed and went up the hill back of the house, planted himself upon the prairie, and was soon lost in sleep. He had not, however, enjoyed the luxury long before he was awakened by a peculiar feeling —something like a person breathing into another's face. Opening his eyes he beheld less than a score of wolves around him. The Captain

JOHN TAPPER

gave a yell (and such a yell as he alone could give) and a bound at the same time for the house, followed by the wolves. But, as usual, he came out victorious, and succeeded in saving himself from destruction by leg bail," according to the 1874 *Andreas* atlas.

Both Colonel John Harrington Stevens and his wife, Frances Miller Stevens, were of Puritan ancestry. Mrs. Stevens died May 15, 1902, of "heart trouble," at age seventy-five. The *Minneapolis Times* article about her gave a relationship, through Puritan grandparents, that made her a second cousin to Henry Ward Beecher, famous Congregational preacher of the 1800s, and to his sister, Harriet Beecher Stowe, American novelist who wrote *Uncle Tom's Cabin*, published in 1852.

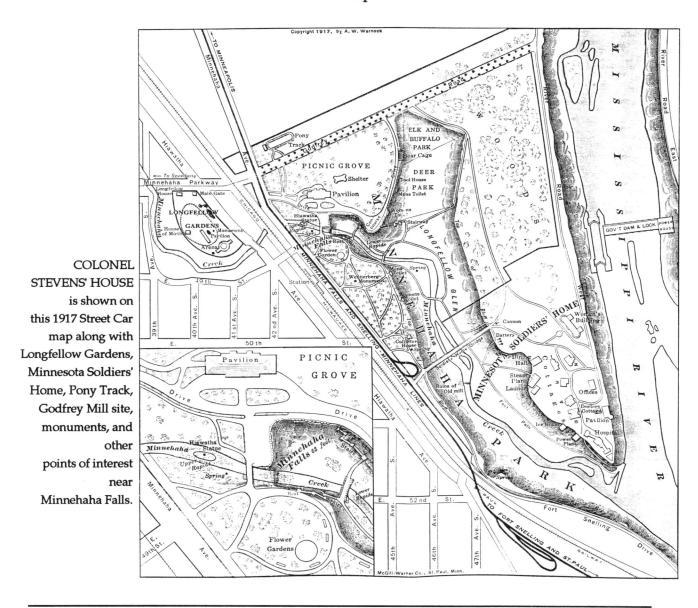

COLONEL STEVENS' HOUSE is shown on this 1917 Street Car map along with Longfellow Gardens, Minnesota Soldiers' Home, Pony Track, Godfrey Mill site, monuments, and other points of interest near Minnehaha Falls.

Chapter 15

Walking Down The Nature Path
Below The Falls

From the falls, there is only about a half mile of creek left until its waters meet the Mississippi River and flow on "from the pine to the palm," as Thoreau put it. The observations that follow were made on a walk along the nature path by Minnehaha Creek, below the falls, on a beautiful August day in 1984. Just downstream from the falls, two teen-age, bikini-clad girls were walking down the creek itself. They had tennis shoes on and were watching out for slippery rocks and extra fast or deep rapids. At one point, they had to grab a tree on an island to catch their balance in the clean, bubbling, sandy stream. Their giggles joined the gurgles of the rapids. Further on, several boys were also reveling in the rapids.

Along the path were sylvan delights such as small, wild sunflowers, daisy fleabane and purple and yellow rocket flowers. Twin sugar maples hung gracefully over the creek, and an elm tree looked close to five feet in diameter at the base; also, there was a cottonwood which was an esti-

BOYS IN THE CREEK
BELOW THE FALLS

mated four feet in diameter at the base and about 125 feet high.

A blue jay was calling from an oak tree, competing with the sounds of redwing blackbirds, warblers and a catbird. There were hackberry trees, currant bushes, grapevines and huge staghorn sumac decorating the path. There was the "beep, beep" of nuthatches and a similar sound coming from the locks on the Mississippi intermittently. Other plants were tall, yellow cone flowers that looked like daisies; burdock, which looked like

THE RAPIDS

BOYS AT PLAY, 1984.

rhubarb; huge willows; aspen; wild roses; Solomon's Seal and ash trees right at the end of a little island in the creek.

The scene was similar to Henry Hunt Snelling's description of the Minnehaha stream and valley below the falls in his *Memoirs of a Boyhood at Fort Snelling* in the 1820s. An excerpt:

Birds were all around me caroling their sweetest notes, the waters danced before me, the wind murmured among the leaves above me with aeolian sweetness, and the flowers around me sent a delicious fragrance to my nostrils.

Next we saw some boys playing at a little spring which runs beside the creek. One of the little Hiawathas told us, "We are Hmong."

A marker informed us that many underground springs break onto the surface of the earth around here and that these underground springs are part of the system that provides water to wells and to the creek. Some of these aquifers, or springs, are as large as great rivers underground, according to the engraved marker supplied by the Minneapolis Park system. We passed the site of a mill built by pioneer Ard Godfrey in the 1850s, and we could see an outbuilding and chimney of the Veterans' Home which was built on the site of Godfrey's home.

We arrived at the mouth of Minnehaha Creek and saw the Mississippi River. As we looked back at the creek from the point formed by the Mississippi and Minnehaha Creek, we were standing to the right of the creek on Godfrey's Point. Suddenly, a little, dark-brown animal the size of a small cat, but with rounded ears and short legs, came out of the brush on the bank and walked along the sand for about five feet. The animal watched us with an

MOUTH OF
MINNEHAHA
Godfrey's Point
is to the right.

arrogant, almost vicious, air; and we remained very still. Then the animal vanished into the bushes and reappeared briefly on a return walk. It had messy, tan whiskers. It was only about fourteen inches long, plus a tail which curved down from the body and almost dragged on the ground. The animal was probably a young woodchuck that had been rooting in the crushed-limestone sand, which made its whiskers tan; but it was not as roly-poly as the traditional woodchuck, or ground hog, pictured in the newspapers on ground-hog day.

Chapter 16

The Godfreys and Their Mills

Ard Godfrey had two mills on the north bank of the creek, the first in 1853. He built his house on the high bluff overlooking the creek and the Mississippi River at the site of the present Veteran's Home. Godfrey's daughter, Harriet, kept a diary and wrote about her pleasant life by the creek, starting in the 1850s. Godfrey was called by sutler Franklin Steele to come from Maine and build a sawmill at St. Anthony in 1848. This mill produced lumber that pushed development of the town of St. Anthony on the east side of the Mississippi and of Minneapolis on the west side. Godfrey was involved in much of the planning and progress of both towns. In 1849 he became the first St. Anthony postmaster.

When she was a girl, Harriet R. Godfrey began her diary about daily life on the raw frontier in Minnesota Territory. She was born in 1849 and lived her earliest years in their house on the east side of the Mississippi near the Falls of St. Anthony. The first Godfrey house still stands and has been restored by the Woman's Club of Minneapolis. Currently, it is at Forty-five Ortman Street, near the intersection of Central and University Avenues North East.

But soon the beautiful glen at Minnehaha prompted Ard Godfrey to make a pre-emption claim on Minnehaha Creek at its mouth on the Mississippi River. With this kind of claim he could settle on public land, with the right to buy it before others. The year of the claim was 1852, and GODFREY'S a claim shanty was soon built on the site. For several years, ten thousand CLAIM dollars was kept hidden in the Godfrey home, in an old green chest, so they could immediately pay for their land when the government requested payment for their claim site. "At that time banks and safes had not been introduced to the West," Harriet Godfrey wrote. The military reservation land, like the Godfrey's claim, needed special legislation, but by 1855 nearly all were satisfied and the claimants got title to their land.

> Note: Re. claim conflicts, Mitchell and Stevens wrote in their 1868 book: "In some instances trouble was made, but the site of a rope attached to a tree was a pretty strong hint how the cat would jump if they did not behave themselves and submit to the rules of the association."

ARD GODFREY''S FLOUR MILL, 1865 Destroyed by fire October 26, 1879. *Courtesy Hennepin History Museum*

The Godfrey land had previously been claimed by Joseph R. Brown, the soldier who made the 1822 exploration of the creek with William Snelling. Brown selected his claim in 1826, but he abandoned it in 1830.

The Godfreys' first improvement to their land was the claim shanty house on the second level of terrace above the creek, and they occupied the house for a while. Later, it was used as housing for lumberjacks at the mill Godfrey built on the creek. The mill was not always open in winter, but there is a notation that the winter of 1857-58 sawmill workers were boarded in the house.

The family's permanent home was built near the top of the hill with a view of both the Mississippi River and Minnehaha Creek. It was a two-story, wooden home that they loved and owned for over twenty years. The Veterans' Home is now on the site. For an exact location, Harriet wrote, "The Woman's building at the Soldiers' Home now marks the spot where the old house stood (as of 1927). The main entrance of the building was at the site of the Godfrey house front door."

Godfrey's 1853-built sawmill was on his land up Minnehaha Creek a bit from his house. Soon, slightly downstream, he built a mill with stones for grinding grain. There was a limestone dam and a raceway carried waterpower to the sawmill. Both mills used water wheels. One of the most popular things the sawmill turned out besides lumber was wood slabs, the rounded outside, full-length part of a log when it was sawed into boards. Farmers used the slabs for roofing, shanties and stables.

In their large home, the Godfrey family did a lot of entertaining, but not fancy entertaining. People from St. Paul came by horse and buggy, and it took a day to reach Minneapolis and the Godfrey house. Then, sometimes, people would visit from three days to a week. There was no nearby store, or freezer, to run to for food, and Mrs. Godfrey made just about everything her family ate, used or wore. All their water came from Minnehaha Creek at first—later from a windmill pump.

On Saturday, food was prepared for Sunday so they would not have to work on the Sabbath. Mrs. Godfrey was of Puritan descent.

Harriet Godfrey had mostly pleasant memories of her childhood by the creek. There were exceptions, however. She was accidentally hurt by a shovelful of stones thrown by a man working on the road at the top of the bluff by her home. It was quite serious, and she had scarring for years from a deep cut. Once she ran across a plank that went over the mill raceway, leaned over to look in the water, and next she found herself under the water. Her brother Abner rescued her.

She had a swing in the trees by her house; and a tree on the bank at nearby Godfrey's Point, where the steamboats tied up, was called The Steamboat Tree. Her father also built a wharf where the steamboats tied up.

When winter and deep snow came, the Godfreys usually stayed home. Travel by horse and buggy to town was a long, cold journey.

One summer day Harriet's mother sent her and two of her sisters down to the shores of Minnehaha Creek to gather the abundant thoroughwort, or boneset, herb, so that it could be dried, with other herbs, for medicine. It was a rule that the girls were not to cross the creek, but the best boneset was on the other side and they decided to wade across barefoot. Their arms held huge quantities of the herb when they were ready to return, so they tucked their hand-knit stockings into their shoes, tied them together, and tried to throw them across the creek. Their throwing attempts fell short of the other bank, and two pairs of shoes and stockings, filled with water, sank and were never recovered.

IDAHO GOLD RUSH

In 1862 and 1863 the head of the household, Ard Godfrey, went west with a party that was seeking gold, among other business interests, leaving his only son, Abner, in charge of the family. Ard went with the Fisk expedition to the Rocky Mountains. At Bannock City, Idaho, he staked a gold claim and built a small lumber mill, using waterpower from mountain springs. Always the millwright, he reported that the crank and shaft of the water wheel were fashioned from heavy wagon axles. Godfrey planned to bring home at least a little gold dust and money from his share of the mill, according to one of his letters.

Godfrey was beyond the scene of both the Civil War and warring between some of the Dakotas and the government. One letter to his wife expressed the belief that it was "Divine Providence" that he left for the west when he did as, otherwise, their only son might have gone into the army; and they would have had more to worry about than they had with Godfrey in the wild west.

After the children were in bed, Mrs. Godfrey frequently spent the evening writing a letter to her husband in Idaho. She wrote, "I often get the blues." One letter was twenty pages, and she put two three-cent stamps on it but was not sure that was enough. Her husband, Ard, returned from the west August 9, 1863.

Young Harriet and her mother and five sisters sewed a lot. They made dresses, such as a green merino dress, and they even sewed such items as a horse blanket. When they had a goose, Harriet had to help pluck it. Abner Godfrey first went to school in the parlor of the Philander Prescott house, as the Prescotts were neighbors to the Godfreys.

Late in 1869, the Godfreys had a party for friends and family at their house. About forty people attended, including a dozen from Richfield, a Frank Langley and three Blaisdell girls. Charlie Roberts and John Moffett were fiddlers for the dance, and music and laughter rang through the Minnehaha gorge.

In October, 1871 the Godfrey family moved to Minneapolis. Harriet regretted leaving her much-loved home for the unknown privileges of town. That fall there was a wonderful Indian summer, Harriet's favorite **MOVE TO** season; the foliage by the creek was "dazzlingly glorious, and the air soft **MINNEAPOLIS** and balmy," she wrote, "and everything is seen through a smoky haze." They moved to a house on the corner of Eighth Street and Eighth Avenue South in Minneapolis, then on the edge of town. In later years Harriet lived on Harriet Avenue near Lake Street.

Chapter 17

The Veterans' Home
Formerly Called the Soldiers' Home

On the bluff above the mouth of Minnehaha Creek, stands a cluster of buildings comprising the Minnesota Veterans' Home, formerly called the Soldiers' Home and, informally, the Old Soldiers' Home. The location is on Godfrey's Point and was the site of Ard Godfrey's house. After the Godfrey family left their beloved home at the mouth of the creek and moved to town in 1871, the family retained ownership of the property for quite a few years. By 1887, the city of Minneapolis had acquired the fifty acres of land at the junction of Minnehaha Creek with the Mississippi and northward for nearly one-half mile—the Godfrey home property. Minneapolis Mayor A.A. Ames wrote the following letter in which he offered the land as a site for the Soldiers' Home:

Minneapolis, Mn.
June 21st, 1887

Hon. H. A. Castle
Chm. Soldiers' Home Com.

Dear Sir

On behalf of the people of the City of Minneapolis, I offer as a site for the proposed Minnesota Soldiers' Home a tract of Fifty (50) acres of land in the city of Minneapolis. Situation the west bank of the Mississippi River near Minnehaha Falls and valued at seventy five thousand ($75,000) dollars. If the proposition is accepted I feel authorized in stating that the said grounds will be connected with the present Park System of Minneapolis and St. Paul in such a manner as to make it the most attractive and beautiful spot in this State.

Very respectfully,
(signed) A. A. Ames
Mayor

At their July 12, 1887, meeting, the Soldiers' Home Committee Board of Trustees accepted the land offer. Therefore, the fifty thousand dollars that had been allocated by the government for land could be added to the building funds. On February 14, 1888, an architect was asked to make plans for four "cottages" and a heating plant, and by the following year,

SOLDIERS' HOME FROM THE RIVER BETWEEN THE TWIN CITIES, MINN.

the first unit of the home was complete. August 13, 1889, the commandant was instructed to transfer the residents to the new Soldiers' Home and close up their temporary housing.

The original Soldiers' Home, built in 1888-89, of red brick, is now gone; but several similar red brick buildings remain today, along with some white stucco ones of more recent vintage. At the turn of the century, steamboats were still docking below the home at the levee on Godfrey's point just as they did when the Godfrey family lived there.

The foliage in the creek glen below the home is thick in summer, and all one can see of the Veterans' Home from the creek is a huge, round chimney and a shed. In the vicinity, there is an impressive, one-arch steel bridge overhead in the trees. Built in 1908 at a cost of forty thousand dollars, the bridge was originally for light vehicular and pedestrian traffic. Some years ago, one could drive a car over the bridge, but now it is blocked off for vehicles. It is still open to strolling veterans and other pedestrians.

The home is on a picturesque site, almost a part of Minnehaha Park. It is approximately two miles from Fort Snelling, across the river from St. Paul and in the city limits of Minneapolis. William Herrick, an ex-soldier who became known as the hermit of Minnehaha Falls, lived at the home for a short time when it was still called the Soldiers' Home. He recorded some details about it in 1903.

VETERAN'S HOME
1910 Postcard
Note two steamboats at the mouth of the creek. The steeple is on the old head-quarters building, which in the old days was the commandant's residence and office.
Courtesy Margaret Bevan

Herrick wrote that there were about fifteen buildings of red brick, and of these, there were five cottages, a dining hall, hospital, pavilion, administration building, two steam plants and others, such as barns. The beautiful lawn and flowers were kept up by residents of the home.

In the pavilion, "entertainments" were sponsored by the Woman's Relief Corps. Soldiers were detailed to work in the dining hall, with each working one week as a waiter or dishwasher. The hospital employed five female and six male nurses, all outsiders. For laundry work, five outsiders were employed, and they were assisted by three residents. Officers in charge were Commandant James Compton, Adjutant McKusic, Quartermaster Straub, Chaplain Smith and Surgeon Bissel.

Residents greeted visitors warmly, and, wrote Herrick, "no one ever leaves the ground without a thrill of gratitude for the courteous and kind treatment shown by the old boys of '61."

FORT SNELLING SOLDIERS, ARMED WITH RIFLES AND A BUGLE(!), SCOUTING IN MINNEHAHA CREEK CANYON, 1898
Courtesy Hennepin History Museum

IV

MINNEHAHA TODAY

Chapter 18

Minnehaha Today

HEALTH BENEFITS FROM WATERFALLS AND THE NATURAL ENVIRONMENT

In the last few years, scientists have collected convincing evidence that people's blood pressure, brains, bodies—and even their blood cells—can receive beneficial effects from a pleasing environment. This brings the realization that creek-lovers' appreciation of time spent at the creek does not come only from imagination or nostalgia but from real physical benefits.

CREEKS *CAN* DISAPPEAR

With all the good that comes from Minnehaha Creek, people hope that it will be preserved for future generations. Creeks *can* disappear. Charles Kuralt, telling about a trip back to his childhood home in North Carolina, said that the nearby creek, where he played as a boy, was completely filled in and gone. At home, Bassett's Creek flows out of Medicine Lake to Minneapolis where it has been diverted underground on the near northside. A few years ago, visitors to the building at Eighth Avenue and north First Street could catch a glimpse of it through an opening in the floor. The opening was later glassed over and has since been closed. BASSETT'S CREEK

When this writer questioned a St. Paul Park and Recreation man about metro creeks that have virtually disappeared—and revealed my Minnehaha Creek book project—he said, "Who's trying to get rid of Minnehaha Creek?" We both laughed and agreed, "No one, yet."

Battle Creek in St. Paul remains a surface stream from Battle Creek Lake to McKnight Road, and then the creek flows through flumes, underground pipes and on the surface, according to a St. Paul man who works on park design and construction. He added, "In Battle Creek park, although the majority of the water flows through an underground storm sewer, there is also a surface flow maintained so we still have a creek." BATTLE CREEK

Source waters of Hidden Falls in St. Paul are also partly underground today. South of the Ford Assembly plant, Hidden Falls was formerly fed by springs and surface drainage, but over the years development has forced source waters underground. Now water for the falls issues from pipes west of Mississippi River Boulevard and then drops several times above ground, until it flows through Hidden Falls Park to the Mississippi below the Ford dam. HIDDEN FALLS

Around the turn of the last century, Bridal Veil Falls was the centerpiece of a beautiful picnic glen that was nearly as popular as Minnehaha Falls. Today the falls is a bit difficult to spot and accessible only to the spry visitor who can lean far over the guardrail or climb down the dirt path beside the culvert bridge on East River Road, near the Franklin Avenue bridge, Minneapolis.

BRIDAL VEIL FALLS

Otto Schussler, the St. Louis Park miller's son, told about watching the growth of Minneapolis' St. Anthony area, about two miles upriver from Bridal Veil Falls, and how town needs encroached on the creek's watershed. Born in 1873, the miller's son became *Doctor* Otto Schussler who wrote in his 1928 *Riverside Reveries* book that the sizable Bridal Veil stream was reduced to a brooklet as the needs of city life took over, such as tunnels, streets, basements, wells, sewer and water facilities—altering the meadows and woods that fed the stream.

DOCTOR SCHUSSLER

Doctor Schussler remembered with apparent nostalgia that he and his wife and Fairview Hospital School of Nursing students, among others, used to walk down the west bank of the Mississippi, across the Capelen iron bridge (taken down about 1923) to enjoy the Bridal Veil Falls on the east side of the river. The falls was thirty-three feet high then. Schussler liked the "fragrance" of the "smell" of spray, whether it was from a waterfall, mill water wheel or ocean waves, stimuli which he felt could "awaken in all of us thoughts beyond the reaches of our souls."

By 1927 the former pretty falls was only an occasional trickle of water; but a city workman told the doctor that, for a comparatively modest cost, waste water could be brought to a point just above the falls site to renew the cascade. This was eventually done.

Bridal Veil Falls' source waters have changed drastically over the years. Bridal Veil Creek once started in east Minneapolis near the city limits in ponds and swamps; then it flowed across southeast Minneapolis to the falls. Incidentally, a St. Paul man believes that at one time this creek was called Strawberry Creek. As the years went by, more and more of the little creek was put into a culvert, and "some houses were built so close to the culvert that their foundations were built around it," according to a May 28, 1961, *Minneapolis Tribune* article. Culvert waters had been diverted in 1952 into storm sewers, mingling with clean waters from industrial processing, air conditioning and street and lawn run-off—then to Bridal Veil Falls.

In 1961 any remaining natural and culvert source waters for Bridal Veil Falls were scheduled to be rerouted for the interstate freeway across the Mississippi. Luckily, an outcry by the right people saw that this did not happen; and the slightly-shortened falls continues its year-round flow, as it has throughout much of local recorded history. In June, 1990, after a lot of rain, Bridal Veil Falls was gushing, at its original site, out of a culvert onto a rock cliff where lacy patterns of water formed a veil that cascaded into a ruffled, rock-strewn "train" of water, which streamed down a ravine for two hundred feet into the Mississippi.

Except for the loss of the falls at Penn Avenue and some channel changes, Minnehaha Creek has escaped *civilizing* to quite an extent. A few, short culverts shadow its waters; but after a good rainfall, the creek is still a pleasant, living stream, bordered by greenery.

PROPOSED LAND CHANGES BY THE FALLS

Sometime in the future, if the current plan is followed, a highway replacing Hiawatha will run under Minnehaha Park; so that the park and the land of the former zoo will be connected. Under present environmental rules, Minnehaha Creek would be affected very moderately, if at all. Completion of this highway construction could very well take ten years; so there is still time to get out to Minnehaha Park and see the lay of the land as it was when colorful Fish Jones lived there in his Longfellow House and hawked the attractions of his zoo.

A Perusal of the Park and Recreation Board's
Master Plan for Minnehaha Park, Dated Winter, 1989-1990

The park board's planning booklet for upgrading Minnehaha State Park anticipates the tunnel solution to the location of Hiawatha Avenue, and plans are under way to proceed with improvements to roads, bridges, pathways, buildings and, eventually, a new entrance. Open space, signage, landscaping and things of historic significance will continue to be preserved or improved.

Major improvement work, on hold since 1967 when the Department of Transportation attempted to buy twenty-three acres of the park to make Hiawatha Avenue a highway, can now go forward. The Highway Department won their case of the right to eminent domain, but public opinion held back a final decision until one of at least five plans, proposed by consulting firms, was accepted by both sides. The report states:

HIAWATHA AVENUE PROJECT

> In 1986 a plan which showed a land bridge and tunnel was approved and partially funded. The first of three segments to be developed is presently under construction. This segment between East 31st Street and east 46th Street is expected to cost eleven million dollars. The remaining segments are estimated at 69 million dollars to be funded through federal, local and state sources.

There is a fund of 53 million dollars which was set aside by the Federal government in 1974 for Hiawatha Avenue~Highway 55 construction.

From the many plans proposed for rerouting Hiawatha Avenue, the one chosen provides for the new Hiawatha corridor to have a grade-separated intersection, in the form of a covered road, over Hiawatha at Minnehaha Parkway. The latter parkway, it appears, will run over the covered road or land bridge, which bridge will also serve to unite the old Longfellow Garden zoo land and the rest of Minnehaha Park. Minnehaha Creek will be under a regular bridge in two places, according to a 1989 engineering drawing.

The proposed Hiawatha covered-highway construction will made it necessary to move the Longfellow House. The new site is to the east. After the move, it now needs utility hookups and rehabilitation. The Longfellow House Restoration Group is in the area to assist in raising funds and repairing the charming old house—as this has been their aim for several years. One of the Society's members recalls the coziness of the house when she used to sit and read on a window bench while the house was used as a library from 1937-67.

MINNEHAHA
PARK In 1988 Minnehaha Park had 529,200 visitors. The park is really used over its capacity, and in a 1989 report about reservations made for Saturdays and Sundays in June, July and August, prime times were reserved one hundred percent of the time.

According to the Summer, 1992, "Minnehaha Park Renovation Plan" and a Fall, 1993, "People for Parks News" booklet, all of Minnehaha Park will be restored close to its natural landscape. Roads and parking lots will be on the perimeter of the park; and historic buildings, bridges, sculptures and other facilities will be brought back to their former charm.

ARBORETUM An arboretum has been suggested, and this would be significant since there used to be a greenhouse and outdoor gardens near the old hotel that was across from the little depot, as recorded by Esther Clark in her diary for 1879 and as quoted in the "Minnehaha Falls" chapter herein.

According to the park board report, virtually the last major improvements at Minnehaha Park, outside of repairs and maintenance, took place in the 1930s when the park's work force was aided by Works Progress Administration (WPA) workers. They built roads, picnic tables, stone bridges, stairs and restrooms. However, numerous smaller projects have taken place since the 1930s. The 1905-built refectory was remodeled, pedestrian bridge approaches repaired and such things as grills and picnic tables added. Although maintained over the years, many of the park's conveniences for the public need repair, upgrading or replacement.

In general, the long-range master improvement plan calls for preserving and protecting natural features of the park, providing access for vehicles, people and bicycles, reinforcing things of historical significance, improving and linking park trails with outside trails, upgrading existing facilities for public use, developing added recreational areas and shielding the park from the noise and distractions of roads or undesirable land uses.

Recruitment of a citizens' advisory board is planned to represent the interests of the neighborhood, Twin Cities residents and tourists from various parts of the United States. There will also be a technical advisory board, made up of people skilled in environmental, historical and geological needs of the park. Also included on this latter board would be agencies such as representatives from the Minnehaha Creek Watershed District, Tourist and Public Works departments and other concerned branches of government.

The natural features of the park—such as the trees, falls, gorge and views—have always attracted people. Added to this are man-made amenities such as the picnic pavilion and adjacent grounds, the Wabun group picnic area, and places to play football, soccer and softball. Any improvements will consider *conservation,* a key word in the park plan, which contains the resolution that "Consideration of the surrounding resources will be a major factor in the park's redevelopment."

Many would like to see a steady flow over the falls for at least three summer months; but the creek and falls are mainly dependent on any water let through the dam at Lake Minnetonka or on rainfall. Pumping of groundwater is out for the foreseeable future. An April 11, 1990, *Star Tribune* article said the Department of Natural Resources had turned down many requests for permits to pump groundwater into metro lakes, and, in fact, the state may decide to permanently prohibit such groundwater pumping to conserve water resources, which have decreased due to dry years and pumping. According to the park board report, water in Minnehaha Creek can be increased by using a series of water pumps and tunnels which can bring water from the Mississippi into the Chain of Lakes and to an outlet, or spillway, of Lake Harriet at its parkway and

THE FALLS AFTER A SUBSTANTIAL RAIN JULY 27, 1990 An exceptionally rainy summer in 1993 kept the creek full brim to brim and made the falls an especially popular spectacle.

Forty-eighth Street South. It has been found that by the time the water travels the distance to the falls, most of it is lost from percolation and evaporation.

Minnehaha State Park is Minnesota's first state park and one of the most popular regional parks in the state. It is on the National Register of Historic Places and is known as the Minnehaha Historic District. The grand total of funds needed for the current, proposed park upgrading project is $7,109,500. The first $1 million request for 1991 and similar funding for 1992 were approved by the legislature, the park board secretary reported. With the careful planning of the park board and adequate funding, the beautiful park by Minnehaha Creek and the Mississippi River appears to have a great future ahead.

PROBLEM GROUND WATER WILL BE CLEANED AND PURIFIED AND RELEASED INTO THE CREEK IN ST. LOUIS PARK

Contaminated ground water under one area of St. Louis Park will be purified to drinking water quality and discharged into Minnehaha Creek at a rate of 120 to 190 gallons a minute under a ground water cleanup plan proposed in late 1989 by the Minnesota Pollution Control Agency. A large St. Louis Park corporation will pay for the million-dollar-plus cleanup project and comply with state air and water quality standards. Since December, 1988, an interim plan has been used.

Pollutants will be processed out by pumping the water up into a high, narrow tower and aerating it with a fan, so that the unwanted chemicals will evaporate as the water trickles down (called air-stripping). A carbon filter will be used at the top of the tower to catch any airborne pollutants; and the water quality will be monitored regularly for thirty years.

The pure water will flow over rocks into the creek and will actually improve the creek waters it joins. The added water supply would not cause flooding as it would be only about one percent of the volume of the creek. Government agencies and the public agreed the plan would be beneficial to the creek, and work on the project is scheduled to begin in the spring of 1990. The discharge will keep the water in the creek's watershed instead of the sewer system. As of April 18, 1990, a Minnesota Pollution Control Agency engineer said the project is "going into construction *now.*"

FIGHTING THE THREATS OF PURPLE LOOSESTRIFE AND EURASIAN WATER MILLFOIL WEED

Purple loosestrife weeds are on the banks of Minnehaha in some places in 1990, and that means trouble! The plant, originally from Europe, has no natural enemies in North America, and the danger is that purple loosestrife can crowd out important vegetation needed by wildlife. In 1989, certain European beetles were being tested to see if they would eat just the loosestrife and leave the desirable vegetation alone.

The purple flowers of the plant are very attractive when they bloom in July and August, but it is a menace. Spraying with chemicals does not kill the plant as it comes back the next year. People from the U.S. Department of Agriculture, the Department of Natural Resources and Hennepin Parks are all currently working on the problem in Minnesota—where an estimated thirty-four thousand acres are infested with the plant. Mechanical or hand removal are options.

Around August 3, 1989, two inspectors, who were looking for purple loosestrife in Minnehaha Creek, reported to authorities that they found a patch of the dreaded noxious weed, Eurasian water milfoil, in Minnehaha approximately three-hundred feet north of the creek passageway under Highway 494. The weed can grow a new plant from only a one-inch fragment; and if the weed is not stopped, or controlled, it has the potential to cause a clogging and flooding in the creek, which is a natural drainage system for a large area in western Hennepin County.

In recent years, the Minnehaha Creek Watershed District, the Department of Natural Resources (DNR), Hennepin County Parks and a private weed control company have been working on the problem. The DNR wanted to prevent the weed from reaching the Mississippi. In 1992, the weed had reached Minnehaha and the Mississippi.

WAYNE M. HOWELL Minneapolis Artist paints a narrow falls framed by late summer foliage. 1989

THE FALLS AND GORGE ARE STILL PICTURESQUE TODAY

The creek, falls and gorge are a pleasant sight today, and the spot where Minnehaha joins the Mississippi is more picturesque today than in the old days, according to architect Walter Stone Pardee. He wrote in his diary that he saw the falls area in its natural state in the 1860s and around 1900 when "the public, careless, dirty, reckless and sinister, invaded the spot," and he saw it in the 1920s when it was a clean "play spot." In 1890, he waded with his sons, down the creek from the falls to the river, and he reported that in 1921 "where brook-river meet, acres of lowland are being filled for park and paths; and this will finish the connection and make a fitting end to the famous brook."

In late summer, 1989, Minneapolis artist Wayne M. Howell, was absorbed in painting a picture of a narrow Minnehaha Falls, framed by foliage.

A CREEK LOVER'S POEM FROM 1889

Minnehaha Falls inspired Emily Ross Peary to create a little poetry booklet about the falls. Mrs. Peary was mentioned in Chapter 13 herein as being the godmother of Henry Longfellow Wickenburg, who lived near the falls. She requested, and received, permission from the Minneapolis Park Board to sell her *Minnehaha Laughing Water* poetry booklet at the falls in 1891 and for a number of years thereafter, although the board rarely allowed such sales. Her 1889 poem referred to "living waters" in regard to veterans at the Soldiers' Home, and the last stanza included a plea that Minnehaha would stay an active stream in the future. An excerpt:

> O'er thy hills of lovely verdure
>   Stands the dear old soldiers' home;
> Men who fought for home and country,
>   For the cause they loved alone,
> Shouldered arms and left their loved ones
>   In the keeping of their God.
> Some have gone where battles never
>   Come to those whose feet have trod
> Paths, that lead to living waters,
>   Where no battles and no dangers
> To the faithful ever come.
>
> So we leave thee, Minnehaha;
>   Thousands more will come and go
> and will love thee, dashing water,
>   Spirit bride and purest daughter,
> Robed in white like frozen snow;
>   May "Our Father" keep thee ever,
> In thy course unto the river,
>   Thou art ever fair to view,
> So we bid you, Minnehaha,
>   "Au revoir," a fond adieu.

V
CHRONOLOGY AND BIBLIOGRAPHY

A Creek Chronology

1822, May - Joseph R. Brown and William Joseph Snelling explore Minnehaha Creek and discover Lake Minnetonka.

1826 Joseph Brown makes the first claim in Minnesota, at the mouth of Minnehaha Creek.

1833 A Doctor Harris arrives on the steamboat *Warrior* and writes an article which describes the falls area.

1849 Mary Eastman calls the creek's falls "Mine-hah-hah," or "laughing waters," in her book *Dahcotah*.

1851 Simon Stevens and Calvin Tuttle travel up Minnehaha Creek by boat and note a cascade between Minnehaha Falls and Lake Minnetonka— probably at the present Penn Avenue. Trip recorded in manuscript account by Louise Burwell.

1852 April - Simon Stevens and Calvin Tuttle travel over land and "discover" their mill site at the present Minnetonka Mills.

1852 June - Simon Stevens, Governor Ramsey and a party of men go up Minnehaha Creek in two bateaux to Lake Minnetonka. Governor Ramsey names Lake Minnetonka during his stay at Simon Stevens' cabin.

1852 Summer, Writer Elizabeth Ellet and party visit Simon Stevens' cabin and explore Lake Minnetonka.

1852 Mary Eastman's poem, "The Laughing Waters," and Seth Eastman's Minnehaha Falls picture are published in *The Iris, An Illustrated Souvenir*.

1852 Ard Godfrey builds a claim dwelling at the mouth of Minnehaha Creek.

1852 September - Col. John Owens and party go overland to Simon Stevens' cabin and Lake Minnetonka.

1852 Fall - The mill carpenters are working on a rough boarding-house at the site of Minnetonka Mills.

1853 March - The sawmill is finished at the site of Minnetonka Mills.

1853 May - The sawmill at the future Minnetonka Mills starts lumber production.

1853 The Minnetonka Hotel is built at the site of Minnetonka Mills.

1853 Ard Godfrey builds a sawmill below Minnehaha Falls near the mouth of the creek, and a few years later, he builds a flour mill below it.

1854 The Stevens and Tuttle sawmill burns at the site of Minnetonka Mills.

1854 Richfield Mills is built.

1855 The Minnetonka Mills sawmill is rebuilt, with a furniture factory upstairs.

1855 Henry Wadsworth Longfellow publishes the poem-book *Song of Hiawatha*. The falls become widely known as Minnehaha Falls.

1855 Francis A. Shaw's poem, "Minnehaha," appears in the book, *Genius of the West*.

1856 *The Minnehaha, or Laughing Water Polka* by Francis H. Brown is published.

1857 The Mill that became Edina Mills is built. Some accounts claim 1856.

1857 Financial panic.

1857 Hezekiah Atwood, manager of the Minnetonka Mills saw mill and furniture factory, falls into Lake Minnetonka while buying logs—dies from pneumonia.

1858 Minnesota is admitted to the Union as the thirty-second state.

1859 October 18 - Nathaniel Butterfield of the Minnetonka Mills area mill drowns when a large sailboat capsizes in rough weather.

1860   The Minnetonka City (Mills) furniture factory closes. Sawmill continues as a reduced and uncertain business.

1861   June - Henry David Thoreau comes to Minnesota and visits Minnehaha Park and Falls, among other places.

1862   The local war between some of the Dakotas and the government starts. Creek explorer Joseph Brown is wounded in the battle of Birch Coulee.

1868,   June - The sawmill at the site of Minnetonka Mills, called the Foster mill at the time, is destroyed by fire.

1869   Thomas Hooker Perkins purchases the Minnetonka Mills sawmill site and builds a flour mill there.

1869   Winter - A near-fatal accident occurs under Minnehaha Falls when photographer Charles Zimmerman is knocked unconscious by a huge icicle.

1874   The Globe Mill (later called Schussler's Mill) is built at Excelsior Boulevard and the creek.

1874   The Minnetonka Mill Company is formed from the mill business started by Perkins and sold, in 1871, to H. M. Vroman and E. H. Hedderly. Charles Burwell becomes manager under owners Loring Fletcher and Charles Loring.

1874   The St. Albans Mill is built three-quarters of a mile downstream from the Minnetonka Mill by John Alt and Company.

1875   The Minnehaha, or Princess, Depot is built on the edge of future Minnehaha Park.

1879,   October - Ard Godfrey's flour mill near the mouth of the creek burns down.

1880-90 Ten-foot, or more, waterfall still at Penn Avenue.

1881   The St. Albans Mill is dismantled.

1882   Probable date when Charles Burwell asks the Minneapolis and St. Louis Railroad to call the mill town Minnetonka Mills instead of "Minnetonka," which had confused passengers on the train.

1883   Charles Burwell has a steamer, Fresco, running between the Minnetonka Mills millpond and Lake Minnetonka.

1883   The Burwell House is built at Minnetonka Mills.

1884   Milling ceases at Minnetonka Mills.

1886   Milling ceases at Richfield Mills.

1888   The Minnesota Soldiers' Home is built by the mouth of the creek at the site of Godfrey's House.

1889   The Minneapolis Park Board purchases land for Minnehaha State Park.

1892   Henry Brown buys the Edina Mills land and Craik's land at the site of today's Edina Country Club.

1893   Antonin Dvorak writes Indian Lament, inspired by the beauty of the falls.

1895   Some of the mill machinery of the Minnetonka Mill is dismantled and sold.

1896   School children and eight horses pull the Stevens House to Minnehaha Park.

1897   Dam on Minnehaha Creek is moved from the "Mills" to Grays Bay outlet to creek.

1897   The Minnetonka Mills building is sold to S. G. Neidhardt, who turns it into a grist, breakfast food and feed mill, run by a steam engine.

1898   Schussler's St. Louis Park mill is dismantled.

1900-20 Creek swimmin' holes on Minnehaha Creek at the island in the creek by the Terwilleger house, Xerxes and York Avenues, Pleasant Avenue and Portland Avenue.

1901   S. G. Neidhardt moves the Minnetonka Mill building and his machinery to southeast Minneapolis.

1902 December - Neidhardt's mill (the former Minnetonka Mill) burns down into ashes and scrap iron on Christmas day, at its relocation site in southeast Minneapolis.

1903 The man called The Hermit of Minnehaha Falls, William Herrick, is about to move away to Wisconsin.

1905 The rustic bridge, carved by Peter Joseph Winnen, around the turn of the century, is still popular.

1906 Most of the animals in the small zoo at Minnehaha Park are sold or given away.

1906 Fi*sh* Jones begins building his Longfellow House replica and Longfellow Gardens zoo near Minnehaha Falls.

1907 Jones opens his Longfellow Zoological Gardens.

1911 Jacob Fjelde's statue of Hiawatha and Minnehaha is placed above the falls.

1914-24 Improvements made at Lake Nokomis, adjacent to Minnehaha Creek.

1916 United States Geological Survey includes information on the falls area.

1917 Hiawatha Festival is put on by the Edina School at the millpond.

1921-55 Except for World War II years, Minnehaha Tourist Camp operating at Minnehaha Park.

1932 Edina mill is torn down.

1934 Longfellow Gardens zoo is dismantled by the city and park board.

1938 Pumps and wells (7) are installed and start to raise Lake Minnetonka's level. Pumps are mostly unused after 1942.

1964, June - President Lyndon Johnson visits Svenskarnes Day and Minnehaha Falls at Minnehaha Park.

1976 Bicentennial American Freedom Train is on display on tracks at the Falls.

1979 One of the customary, yearly creek cleanups by the Izaak Walton League fills two dump trucks.

1990 Lake Minnetonka residents urge resumption of pumping to increase the lake's level.

1990s Plans call for Hiawatha Avenue corridor to run under a portion of Minnehaha Park land, thus connecting the old zoo site to the park. The fight against Purple Loosestrife and Eurasian Water Milfoil weeds continues. Minnehaha Park is the subject of a $7 million master plan to improve and add facilities in the upcoming years. Contaminated ground water under one area of St. Louis Park will be purified to drinking water quality and enter the creek at a rate of 120 to 190 gallons a minute and will be monitored for thirty years.

Bibliography

INTERVIEWS

Dorn, Ada Mayhew, 1988 and 1990 personal interviews re. creek memories.

Ennenga, Mark, 1988 phone conversation re. cleaning up Minnehaha Creek by the Izaac Walton League.

Ford, Eugene, 1989 telephone and letter interviews about creek memories in south Minneapolis. Now of southern Minnesota and genealogists, the Fords bought a copy of this book for their genealogy club's library.

Foster, Marion, a Wickenburg relative, and a member of the Longfellow House Restoration Society. Mrs. Foster also furnished the tourist camp information saved by her mother, Mrs. Katie Edmunds.

Gervais, Marlys, phone interview re. her personal story of the Portland swimming hole. She is now an Edina resident, and this is her maiden name.

Guiney, Dorothea, Site Director in 1988, The John H. Stevens House, Minneapolis, Minnesota.

Hennepin County Pioneer Association, Long Lake, Minnesota. Conversations with curators A. Stubbs and Jim Roehl and other members.

Lacy, Lyn, Minneapolis, Media Specialist, teacher and free-lance writer. Interview and tour re. her ongoing research of history in the Minnehaha Falls area.

Lerman, Mary, Horticulturist, Minneapolis Park and Recreation Board, telephone interview about creek bird sanctuary and nesting areas, 1988.

Longfellow House Restoration Group, Sharon Siegrist, Chairperson. Information bulletins, zoo pamphlet of 1928, personal stories of members re. the zoo. Zoo pictures from Jones' 1928 pamphlet which was saved by Agnes Quist, mother of Mrs. Siegrist.

McElroy, Wyllys, personal and telephone interviews. He furnished Davison's map, 25 Miles Around Minneapolis, 1881 corrected to 1884. Interviews 1988, 1989.

Minnehaha Creek Watershed District, phone inquiries 1987-90. Also Minnehaha Creek Canoeing Map and creek engineering facts, including management and water levels of Lake Minnetonka.

Minnesota Pollution Control Agency, St. Paul, Minnesota. Phone inquiries re. the St. Louis Park Minnehaha Creek water purification project in the last chapter of this book. They sent a Minnesota Pollution Control Agency fact sheet, with a project drawing, dated November, 1989.

Ringstad, David, City of Minnetonka Historical Society, re. Minnetonka Mills.

Rodum, David, City of Minnetonka Historical Society, re. Minnetonka Mills.

Schuman, Claudia, Minneapolis suburb, Esther Clark diary material interviews. Minneapolis.

Veteran's Home - 1984 and 1989 inquiries by letter and phone regarding the home.

Vockrodt, Bob, Public Affairs Director, Minnesota Department of Transportation inquiries re. Hiawatha corridor.

Westover, Bonnie, Site Director, 1990, The John H. Stevens House, P.O. Box 17241, Minneapolis, Minnesota, 55417.

Winnen, Peter - conversations with his descendants and information gathered at the Western Hennepin County Pioneer Association, Long Lake, Minnesota. Re. the much-photographed rustic bridge below Minnehaha Falls at the turn of the century.

Wyman, Edwin, Jennie Wyman Smith and Leland Wyman. Personal and telephone interviews re. their family and Minnehaha Creek, Edina, Minnesota.

MANUSCRIPTS
AND UNPUBLISHED SOURCES

Allanson, George G., a grandson of Major Joseph R. Brown, "Brown's Castle, The Most Remarkable Structure of the Minnesota Valley," July 23, 1928, Minnesota Historical Society Archives.

Atwood, Abbie Tuttle, Cook Book, recipes from her notebook, 1857 and a few years after, and her daybook. From Atwood papers, courtesy of Don Andrus.

Bock, Ruth, Courtesy Renee Ubl, From

Longfellow House Restoration Society, *Tales about "Mr. Tails."* Re. Longfellow Gardens zoo and her lion tamer story.

Bodue, Virginia, Editor, *Edina Close Up,* A League of Women Voters of Edina Publication.

Bull, Coates P., handwritten *"Minnehaha Creek,"* from Edina Historical Society archives, refer to m.d. E.H.S. 78.44.11.

Burwell, Charles, letter to the Department of the Census, February 19, 1901. Sources: Leland Wyman collection and the Minnetonka Historical Society archives.

Burwell, Louise, *Minnetonka Mills: Its School Life,* written circa 1921, a Minnesota Historical Society archives manuscript. A Real Find! Miss Burwell writes about an unpublicized scouting trip, by boat, that Simon Stevens and Calvin Tuttle made up Minnehaha Creek to the outlet lake (Grays Bay) in 1851 and about a falls, besides Minnehaha, on the creek at the time. In separate articles by Stevens and Tuttle in *The Excelsior Weekly* of May 30, 1883, both men imply their previous acquaintance with *Minnehaha Creek* before their widely-heralded discovery in April, 1852, of the *beauty* and *extent* of the *lake,* of rumor, that soon became known as Minnetonka. Therefore, Louise Burwell's 1851 date for the men's creek trip of discovery is no doubt correct.

Clark, Esther, 1870s, diary excerpts courtesy Claudia Schuman.

Dvorak, Antonin, information folder at the Minnesota Historical Society.

Dvorak-Kreisler, *Indian Lament.* Used p. 4 of the sheet music from the Minneapolis Public Library.

Edina Library - history file, one Xeroxed copy, reference only. Re. general Edina Mills information and location of Grange Hall.

Eustice, Ella Alma,*"Out of My Mind,"* Edina Historical Society, Refer #75.27.1, J. T. Grimes' daughter's memories, including numerous fish in lake outlet at spawning time.

Fisher, Jill, Project Planner, City of Minnetonka, obtained about March 18, 1988. Information re. the Minnetonka Hotel, built 1853.

Frear, Dana W., *Trails Through Minnetonka Mills,* An undated copy-machine booklet, edited by G. S. Envil, in Minnetonka Library Clipping file. It shows the location, on a map-drawing, of the Stevens and Tuttle dam, and other Minnetonka City early buildings — includes site of old Indian trail.

____, Minnetonka Town,'" A History of the First Hundred Years of Minnetonka, Minnesota," from Minnesota Historical Society archives. This includes the names of the soldiers on the creek trip in Chapter 1, and it also gives the 1901 date for the Minnetonka Mill move to southeast Minneapolis.

Gilmore, Mrs. Perry, daughter of Hezekiah Atwood, a picture of her folks' 1852-built house (more likely 1854) and comments. Courtesy Hennepin County Historical Society.

Hennepin County Historical Society, "Falls" file. Re. Dvorak, from "The Palimpest, March, 1930, Dvorak at Spillville." Also, a cartoon in the files says Dvorak came to the falls September 4, 1893.

Hesler, Alexander, of Chicago, letter to Russell Blakely, from archives of the Minnesota Historical Society. Describes George Sumner's showing of Hesler's Minnehaha Falls picture to Longfellow.

Howe, Leone Wadsworth, drew "Creek Memories" in Chapter 7. Mrs. Howe has common ancestry with Henry Wadsworth Longfellow.

Jarvis, Dr. Nathan S., his hand-written letters of June 1, 1833 and June 18, 1833, Minnesota Historical Society archives. Re. Doctor Harris as probable author of 1833 letter describing the falls area, Chapter 14.

Jenkins, Mrs. S. H., *Jennie Atwood Pratt* brief biography paper, written in 1949 for the Minnesota Historical Society and the Hennepin County Historical Society, from the Western Hennepin County Pioneer Association. Locates Calvin Tuttle's log cabin on west side of the Mississippi, story of drowning of Hezekiah Atwood and family information.

Jensen, Steffen, former director of the Minnehaha tourist camp at Minnehaha Falls for a period of about twelve years, circa 1930. Typed article. Source: M.

Foster, Longfellow House Restoration Group.

Johnson, Betty, Economic Background of Minnetonka, Minnesota, May 1972. Written for the city's *Comprehensive Guide Plan*. It gives the 1901 date for the move of the Minnetonka Mill building to southeast Minneapolis.

Minneapolis Collection of Minneapolis Public Library, history clippings file on Minnehaha Falls. Re. 1911 pump house at Longfellow Gardens pumping 1,200 gallons per minute over the falls, names of soldiers with Brown and Snelling and news clippings.

Minneapolis Park and Recreation Board, *Minnehaha State Park - Master Plan*, Winter, 1989-90.

Minnesota Soldiers' Home Annual Report, published by St. Paul Pioneer Press, 1888. It includes the fact that the Soldiers' Home site was donated, so all funding could be used for building purposes.

Minnetonka Library clippings file, Groveland School, 1854-1952. Typed article states Bayard Shaver was a teacher there and later was Assistant Superintendent of Hennepin County Schools. File also contains booklet *Picturesque Minnetonka*.

Pardee, Walter Stone, his 190-page autobiography, 1922, from the Hennepin County Historical Society.

Report of the Creation, Evolution and Purpose of the Minnesota Soldiers' Home, 1943. Letter of Mayor A. S. Ames of Minneapolis, dated June 21, 1887, offering the donation of fifty acres of land for the proposed Soldiers' Home, to Hon. H. A. Castle, Chairman Soldiers' Home Committee. The offer was accepted.

Richfield Library of Hennepin County History clippings file re. Richfield Mills.

Rodum, David, *The Raymond House - Minnetonka Hotel*, written circa 1987. Also contributed other Minnetonka Mills material.

St. Louis Park History and Clippings File, St. Louis Park Library. Re. factory that allegedly polluted the creek.

Sardeson, Frederick W., *Geologic Atlas of the United States*, Minnesota. Minneapolis-St. Paul Folio, Engraved and published by U.S. Geological Survey, Washington, D.C. 1916.

Shaver, Bayard T., Unpublished manuscript labeled *APPENDIX, Minnehaha Creek and Falls*, courtesy Minnetonka Historical Society. This confirms that a kiln was erected by Craik Brothers, Edina Mills, for "browning or roast-oats," with a "specialty of manufacturing oat meal and pearl barley."

Stevensfest Family Fun Day pamphlet, July 28, 1985, by 1985 Aquatennial, General Mills, Junior League of Minneapolis, Minneapolis Park and Recreation Board, Sponsors.

Wroge, Jeanette E., teacher, Burwell School, *The Mills That Are No More*, from Clippings File at Minnetonka Library, dated May 22, 1964.

NEWSPAPERS

Balcom, Tom, *South Side Journal*, "Park Useage Was Controversial in 1880s, " 1983.

Bromley, Edward A., *Minneapolis Journal*, "Interesting Story of Old Minnetonka Mill," December 29, 1902.

Bull, Coates P., *Edina Morningside Courier*, "Edina . . . Events in 1889," January 17, 1952.

Burke Evelyn, *Minnetonka Herald*, "Grays Bay Dam Nothing to Fool Around With," March 4, 1965.

Butterfield, F.J., Long Lake, Minnesota, *Hennepin County Enterprise*, March 18, 1926, "An Old Settler's Tale of Early Pioneer Life in Minnesota," Contributed by his descendant, R. Avery Stubbs.

Clark Esther, *Minneapolis Star and Tribune*, "Neighbors Past," June 23, 1984. Excerpts from her 1870s diary re. Minnehaha Falls.

Davidson, Diane, *The Highland Villager*, "Longfellow's Lines Left Their Mark on Minnehaha Falls and Park," March 2, 1983. Includes mention of the Snelling duel.

Dawson Jim, *Star Tribune*, "Shaping Modern Minnesota," Metro, September 11, 1988. Re. "Great glaciers carved out Minnesota's lakes, rolling land."

Dobson, Charlie, *St. Louis Park Sun*, "Izaak Walton League Keeps Watch Over Minnehaha Creek," August 17, 1980.

Edgar, Randolph, *The Minneapolis Journal,* Editorial Section, "Minnetonka Mills, Unheeded Now by Motorists, Once Minneapolis' Rival and a Steamboat Port . . . Hennepin County's Garden of Eden Goes Back More Than a Hundred Years to Its Exploration by Joseph Brown and Snelling . . ." June 28, 1925. Courtesy of the Leland Wyman Collection. This helps solve the mystery of why the mill did not function after 1884.

Freeborn, Dan, *Star Tribune,* "Plan Would Purify Contaminated Water, Pump It Into Creek," Fall, 1989.

Furst, Randy, *Star Tribune,* "Park Innovations Answer Needs of a Changing City," January 13, 1990.

Godfrey, Harriet Razada, *The Minneapolis Journal,* "The Diary of the First White Child Born in Minneapolis," March 13,1927.

Gonzalez D., Staff Writer, *Star Tribune,* Officials Ponder Fate of Historic House in Minnetonka Mills," March 10, 1988.

Gray, Dick, *Lake Minnetonka Sun,* "Passwords — Minnetonka and Minnehaha Creek," September 15, 1982.

Hanzlik, K. Darcy, *Minneapolis Star and Tribune,* "Dry Spring Renews Rivalry Over Lake, Creek Water," April 16, 1987, Community - North Hennepin Zone.

Hennepin County Review, Hopkins, Minnesota, "How well do you know your Hopkins History," January 11, 1945. Re. Dr. Otto Schussler, the miller's son, who lived 1873-1949.

___, Edina Mills, May 29, 1924.

Hillinger, Charles, *The Courier-Journal & Times,* Louisville, Kentucky, "Minnehaha Park 'Braves' Fighting Freeway," June 16, 1968. From the Los Angeles Times - Washington Post Service. National article re. the proposed Hiawatha corridor that would infringe on and drown out Minnehaha Falls. It cites the fame of the Hiawatha poem and that Minneapolis has "one of the finest park systems in the nation," while no other U.S. city has as many lakes as Minneapolis.

Hodges, Parker, *St. Louis Park Sailor,* "Rapidly Spreading Weed Found in Minnehaha Creek," August 9, 1989.

Kaplan, Steven, *Minneapolis Star and Tribune,* Sunday Magazine, "Water Everywhere, Lakes of the Twin Cities," July 19, 1987.

Leslie, Frank, *Frank Leslie's Illustrated Newspaper,* December 25, 1869. Article reproduced on a Minnesota History Xerox copy available at Hennepin County Historical Society, Minnehaha file.

Meyer, Ellen Wilson, *Wayzata Weekly News,* "Tales from Tonka," June 6, 1983.

Meier, Peg, *Star Tribune, Variety,* February 9, 1988., Re. Fish Jones and his zoo and Dan Patch.

Minneapolis Journal, "Coney Island Legal Tangle," March 31, 1904. Re. purchase of the Gardner Pavilion by Minnehaha Park.

___, "A Statue for Minnehaha, Suggestion as to Jacob Fjelde's Fine Work That Should Be Carried Out," August 5, 1902.

___, "Falls of St. Anthony in 1833 — An Old Letter in a Portland, Me. Paper at That Date Also Tells of Minnehaha," March 30, 1900.

___, Color Graphic Section, December 24, 1933. Re. pop stands and carnival devices lining entrance to Minnehaha Park in 1907 before condemnation and purchase proceedings.

___, "Fast Ones at 'Haha," July 1, 1901. Re. harness racing.

___, " 'Haha Track Is No More," March 28, 1903.

___, "Advancing City 'Annexes' Frontier Mill That Ground Flour for Indians When Minneapolis Was a Village," April 20, 1924. Includes memories of George Millam, Miller of Edina.

___, by Staff, "Historic Structure Gone," December 26, 1902, 6:1. Re. burning of old Minnetonka Mills building in southeast Minneapolis.

___, "Old Elk is Slain: Young Bucks Fight," December 17, 1912.

___, "Girl Who Left Play for Diary Records 70 Years of History," February 20, 1927 to April 10, 1927, Sundays. Diary of Harriet Godfrey, reference, Minnesota Historical Society, Tuttle Scrapbook, 1921-28 (FF613 M 4T9).

___, "Grass Grows Over Crest of Minnehaha Falls . . . Swimming Holes Vanish," May 26, 1938. Re. Portland and Xerxes swimming holes.

Minneapolis Star Journal Staff, "Minnehaha in

Full Glory Again Recalls Days of Creek Steamers," June 5, 1942.

Minneapolis Star and Tribune, "Minnehaha Falls to Flow for LBJ," June 16, 1964.

The Minneapolis Times, Mrs. John Stevens article, May 16, 1902. Re. Mrs. Stevens' death and her ancestors.

Minnetonka City's second sawmill fire: The debate about the date that the sawmill at Minnetonka City burned down for the second time may never be solved.

D. Rodum of the Minnetonka Historical Society believes that a few secondary sources took the 1860 date of the second sawmill burning from Atwater and Stevens (History of Minneapolis and Hennepin County, Volume III, 1895). There are at least four sources that give, or point to, *1868* as the time of the burning of the sawmill at Minnetonka City for the second time:

The Farmers Union, a grange paper, Minneapolis, July 1868: "The Old Foster saw mill at Minnetonka was burned to the ground on the 8th of June." (This was the complete mention — no other details were given.)

Bayard Shaver, who lived in the vicinity, mentioned the 1857 financial panic and an embezzlement which led to suspending operations (1860). "After this the factory was used but little, and the mill led a meager and uncertain existence, *changing hands several times."*

Edward Bromley, Minneapolis Journal, December 19, 1902 article: "The first lumber was sawed in the mill May 12, 1852 (sic 1853) and the last about *seventeen* years later. The upbuilding of the lumber business at St. Anthony Falls and a fire that swept through the old structure furnished an excuse in 1869 for abandoning the sawmilling project and erecting a flour mill on the original site."

Johnson, Betty, "Economic Background of Minnetonka, Minnesota," written for the city's Comprehensive Guiide Plan, May 1972. "In 1867 the Great Northern Railroad, now the Burlington Northern, was laid across Minnetonka. The St. Albans station was located where Plymouth Road crosses the railroad. A spur line went from there to the mill."

Morris, M., *Minneapolis Star* Staff Writer, "After 10-Year Campaign, Miss Burwell to See Her Dream Church," March 31, 1955.

Nelson, Milton O., *The Weekly Northwestern Miller,* "The Old Minnetonka Mills," November 22, 1899. This helps solve the mystery of the Minnetonka Mills dismantling. Courtesy of the Leland Wyman Collection.

Owens, Col. John P., *The Minnesotian,* St. Paul, Minnesota. "Minnetonka and a Trip Thereto," September 11, 1852. Condensed in Chapter 3.

Percy, Mary Craik, *The Northwestern Miller,* "Today and Yesterday, the Mills of Edina," January 30, 1935, Volume 181, No. 4.

Perkins, Will E., *The Minneapolis Sunday Tribune,* "Early Hopkins is Pictured by Pioneer Citizen," as told to D. W. Frear, September 19, 1929.

Pioneer Press, Feature Section, "Early Editor of St. Paul Pioneer Was Lumberman, Indian Trader, Inventor, Legislator and Establisher of Towns — Brought 'Ox-less Carriage' to State," July 25, 1915. Long, comprehensive autobiography of Joseph Renshaw Brown.

Puckett, Karl, *Wayzata/Plymouth Sailor,* Volume 6, Number 17, "Let the Harvest Begin - Weed fighters to hack Eurasian water milfoil down to size in Lake Minnetonka," July 19, 1989.

Quinn, Krystal, *Minneapolis Star and Tribune* Staff Writer, "House Where Minneapolis Was Born Will be Opened to the Public This Sunday," about July 27, 1985. Re. Stevens House.

Rebuffoni, Dean, *Star Tribune,* "Imported Beetle May Help Attack Pesky Loosestrife," August 7, 1989.

Rybski, John, *Minneapolis Star and Tribune* article, "The City's Secret Waterfalls," Picture Magazine, December 1, 1974.

Schmickle, Sharon, *Minneapolis Star and Tribune,* "Board Seeks Minnehaha Creek Level That Will Wash," Community/South Section, July 22, 1982.

Stubbs, Charles Rolla, *Minnetonka Record,* "Pioneer Reminiscences," March 8, 1907.

Swanson, Merrill, *Minneapolis Morning Tribune,* "Born in a Police Station, He Stayed 'True Blue' 31 Years," October 31, 1958. Used for Wickenburg family stories in the Minnehaha Falls vicinity.

Taliaferro, Lt. Lawrence, *Pioneer and Democrat,* July 11, 1856. Re. Brown's Falls being named for Major General Brown. This paper not available, but the information is in *Minnetonka Beach* by Bergmann Richards, 1955, Minnetonka Beach Civic Association, last footnote, page 19.

Thompson, Ruth, *Minneapolis Tribune*, Minnesota Memories, "Timber Wolves Stalked Men in Pioneer Days," September 16, 1949.

Upham, Daniel, *Minneapolis Tribune* Staff Writer, "Road Engineers Find Way to Save Bridal Veil Falls," May 28, 1961.

Walsh, James, *Minneapolis Star Tribune*, "DNR Will Suspend Pumping Permits, Lakeshore Owners Protest," April 11, 1990.

Way, Ron, *Minneapolis Tribune* Staff Writer, "Minnehaha's Fans Told of Rock Risk," April 29, 1969.

Wood, David A., *Lake Area News*, "Area History, A Minneapolis Pioneer's Journal," May, 1984. Re. the John and Esther Clark family mentioned in the Edina and Minnehaha Falls chapters.

MAPS

Dahl, P. M., Plat of Property in Minnetonka Township, T 117 R 22, Hennepin County, Minnesota, 1898. Reprinted in 1981 by the Minnetonka Historical Society.

Davison, C. Wright, Publisher, *Davison's Map, 25 Miles Around Minneapolis, 1881 Corrected to 1884*, Geo. W. Cooley, Civil Engineer. Shows the six mill sites on Minnehaha Creek.

Hudson's Indexed Map of Minneapolis, 1905 Election Districts, source Minnesota Historical Society Archives. This shows "Red Cedar Lane" between Upton and Sheridan Avenues, which helps identify the 1880-90 picture of a waterfall at Penn Avenue as the second cascade that Stevens and Tuttle saw on their unpublicized trip up Minnehaha in 1851, as recorded by Louise Burwell (Chapter 7).

Minnehaha Creek Canoeing Facilities Map. Prepared by the Minnehaha Creek Watershed District in Cooperation with the cities of Minnetonka, Hopkins, St. Louis Park and Edina Recreation Departments, and the Minneapolis Park and Recreation Board. Circa 1986. It shows portages and identifies various places along the creek.

Wright, Geo., Surveyor, *Map of Hennepin County*, 1873, T. 117, Minnetonka City. Includes location of Paint Shop.

Note: regarding the map-picture-drawing of Minnetonka Mills about 1883, by J. Hallberg, in Chapter 3, the above maps were used plus a hand-drawn Minnetonka Mills historical map by Dana Frear — plus on-the-spot input from Dave Ringstad of the Minnetonka Historical society through a mill area tour.

The Burwell house on the map was reduced from a drawing by Terry Warner, St. Louis Park artist, and the Minnetonka Hotel drawing was reduced from a drawing by Dave Rodum of the City of Minnetonka Historical Society.

PERIODICALS

Balcom, Tom, *The Minnesota Volunteer*, "Minnesota's State Parks Celebrate Their First Century - Our First State Park Was Established 100 Years Ago" [Minnehaha, March 9, 1885] May-June, 1985 issue.

___, *Minnesota History Magazine*, "A Tale of Two Towers, Washburn Park and Its Water Supply," Spring, 1984.

Dunwiddie, Foster W., *Minnesota History Magazine*, "The Six Flouring Mills on Minnehaha Creek," Spring, 1975.

Flanagan, John T., *Minnesota History* quarterly, Volume 16, Minnesota Historical Society, 1935. Re. Thoreau's visit to Minnesota.

Frear, Dana W., *Hennepin County History*, Fall, 1966, "Rural Hennepin County's Early Flour Mills Were Many," No. X in a Historical Series.

Potter, Alan H., *Gopher Historian*, Spring, 1965, "Minnesota's Most Famous Spot, Minnehaha Falls."

Readers Digest, March 1947, "Million Dollar Show-Off [Dan Patch] Pg. 97 re. "The Parson" in frock coat and black derby who scouted and bought the horse.

Southern Minnesota Quarterly, Volume III, Nos. 2 and 3, pgs. 7, 8 and 12. "Frontier Maid Becomes Belle of Capitol Society, Ellen Brown Allanson, Granddaughter of Sioux Chieftain, Attended Inaugural Balls . . ." Article by a Joseph R. Brown descendant. It gives facts on Brown and tells how his daughter attended Lincoln's inaugural ball.

Zalusky, Joseph W., *Hennepin County History*, Fall, 1967, "Fish Jones and His Irresistible Longfellow Gardens."

PUBLISHED SOURCES - BOOKS

Adams, Mrs. Ann, *Early Days of Red River Settlement and Fort Snelling*, 1821-29, Minnesota Historical Society Collections, No. 6, 1894. This was used in Chapter 1 re. Fort punishment methods and the Snelling family.

Allanson, Winona Blanche, *Indian Moons*, Augsburg Publishing House, Minneapolis, 1927. This gives a genealogy of Joseph R. Brown's wife and tells of the gunshot wound which led to their meeting and romance.

Anderson, Gary C., *Little Crow*, Minnesota Historical Society Press, 1986. General background information for Chapter 1.

Andreas, A. T., *Illustrated Historical Atlas of the State of Minnesota*," Published by A. T. Andreas, Chicago, Illinois, 1874. Gives lengthy Joseph R. Brown memorials and other pioneer history.

Atwater, Judge Isaac and Col. John H. Stevens, *Minneapolis and Hennepin County*, Volume II, 1895. Used for Richfield Mills.

___, *History of Hennepin County*, Volume III, 1895. Re. Godfrey's sawmill and the useful slabs — also re. Minnetonka.

Baker, Gen. James H., *Minnesota Historical Society Collections*, Volume XII, 1908, "Address at Fort Snelling in the Celebration of the Centennial Anniversary of the Treaty of Pike With the Sioux."Re. Jos. Brown, p. 298.

Baker, James H., A.M., *Minnesota Historical Society Collections*, Volume XIII, 1908, his book *Lives of the Governors of Minnesota*. Material on Joseph Renshaw Brown.

Blegen, Theodore C., *Minnesota, A History of the State*, University of Minnesota Press, 1963. Indian land cessions — p. 172. J. R. Brown removed as Indian agent under spoils system, pg. 264, and other Brown material.

Bromley, Edward A., Minneapolis, *Portrait of the Past*, Voyageur Press, Inc., Minneapolis, 1973. Originally published 1890. Pictures of Fort Snelling, two of Minnehaha Falls, John H. Stevens house and Nicollet House.

Buck, Daniel, *Indian Outbreaks*, Ross & Haines, Inc., Minneapolis, 1965. Background material for Chapter 1, including Red Thunder, p. 20.

Busch, Richard R., *Report on the Excavation of the Edina Mill (Summer 1977)*. Edina Historical Society.

Case, John H., *Collections of the Minnesota Historical Society*, Volume XV, May 1915, "Historical Notes of Grey Cloud Island and Its Vicinity." This covers Joseph Brown leaving his post at St. Croix Falls and canoeing to Oliver's Grove (Hastings) and lot platting for his log house.

Carley, Kenneth, *The Sioux Uprising of 1862*, The Minnesota Historical Society, St. Paul, 1976.

Castle, Henry A., *Minnesota: Its Story and Biography*, Volume I, 1915. Joseph R. Brown material, including founding Brown's Valley and his steam wagon.

City of Minnetonka Historical Society, *C.H. Burwell, Minnetonka Mills, Minnesota* booklet, 1987.

___, *Minnetonka, A Brief History*, June, 1983, booklet.

___, *Welcome to Historic Burwell House*, built in 1883, one page.

Coggeshall, Wm. T., The Poets and Poetry of the West, "Minnehaha" by Frances A. Shaw, 1860. Previously published, 1855, in *The Genius of the West*.

Commemorative Issue, Various Authors, *Picturesque Minnetonka*, 1976. Minnetonka statistics — Minnetonka Library Clippings File.

Cruikshank, Ernest A., *Jacob Brown - 1775-1828*, Minnesota Historical Society.

Daniels, Dr. Asa W., *Minnesota Historical Society Collections*, Volume XII, 1908, "Reminiscences of Little Crow."

Dunn, James Taylor, *The St. Croix, Midwest Border River*, Minnesota HistoricalSociety, 1965 and 1979. Re. Joseph R. Brown meets H. Schoolcraft on the river. More on this encounter under "Mason, Philip P."

___, *Marine on St. Croix, 150 Years of Village Life*, Marine Restoration Society, 1989. Re.

"The County seat at the north end of present-day Stillwater, then called Brown's Warehouse, was named *Dakotah.*"

Dunsmoor, Irving A., re. 1853, *Old Rail Fence Corners*, Minnesota Historical Society Press, St. Paul, 1976. First edition 1914.

Dykstra, Muriel and Joan Frey, *The Fun and Facts of Lake Minnetonka*, 1977.

Eastman, Charles A., *From the Deep Woods to Civilization*, University of Nebraska Press, 1916.

Eastman, Mrs. Mary, *Dahcotah, Life and Legends of the Sioux*, 1849, reprinted 1962 Ross & Haines, Inc., Minneapoliis. P ii, Introduction: Re. the "Little Falls" that the Indians call Mine-hah-hah, or "laughing waters."

Edgar, Randolph, *Record of Old Boats*, published by W. C. Burton, 1926. P. 10 reference to Burwell's propeller boat, *Fresco.*

Edina Historical Society, *Edina Centennial 1888-1988* calendar booklet, 1987. Pictures and information on Edina, including 1888 building of Edina grade school.

Ellet, Elizabeth F., *Summer Rambles in the West*, New York: J.C. Riker, 1853. Calling Simon Stevens "the hermit," she describes his Minnetonka cabin.

Ellis, S.E., *Picturesque Lake Minnetonka, Official Souvenir, Story and Guide to the Queen of All Inland Lakes*, 1906; republished by Excelsior-Lake Minnetonka Historical Society, 1974.

Folwell, William Watts, *A History of Minnesota, Volume II*, The Minnesota Historical Society, 1961. Gives location of Joseph R. Brown stone mansion on Minnesota River in 1862. Map, p. 117, p. 122, George Allanson located Brown home on "southeast quarter of the northeast quarter of section 8, township 114, range 37" which was in western Minnesota on the Minnesota River.

Ford, Antoinette E. and Neoma Johnson, *Minnesota, Star of the North*, Lyons and Carnahan, Chicago, 1961. Basic Minnesota background material.

Fridley, Russell W. and June Holmquist, *Minnesota's Major Historic Sites*, Minnesota Historical Society, St. Paul, 1963. Minnehaha Depot, Falls, John H. Stevens House, Dakota Land Cessions.

___, A Living Past, 15 *Historic Places in Minnesota*, Minnesota Historical Society, St. Paul, 1973. Pictures of Minnehaha Depot, Upper and Lower Sioux Agency.

Hallberg, Jane, Leone Howe, Mary Jane Gustafson, *History of the Earle Brown Farm*, Brooklyn Historical Society, 1983. Re. Edina's Henry Brown, p. 50.

Hampl, Patricia, *Spillville*, Milkweed Editions, Minneapolis, 1987. Re: Antonin Dvorak.

Hansen, Marcus L., *Old Fort Snelling*, Ross & Haines, 1958. Contains William Snelling duel information.

Harris, W.H. and J.S. Levy, Editors, *The New Columbia Encyclopedia*, Columbia University Press, New York and London, 1975. Reference material such as early cars, propeller boats and phonographs.

Herrick, William, *The Hermit of Minnehaha Falls*, Edited by Samuel A. Hatch, 1903. Includes information on the pony ring and Soldiers' Home.

Hesterman, Paul D., *The History of Edina, Minnesota*, Burgess Publishing, Edina, Minnesota, Edina Historical Society, 1988.

Holbrook, Florence, Principal of Forestville School, Chicago, *The Hiawatha Primer*, Houghton, Mifflin and Company, Boston and Chicago, 1898, The Riverside Press, Cambridge.

Holcombe, Major and Wm. Bingham, *History of Minneapolis and Hennepin County, Minnesota*, 1914. Re. Henry Brown.

Hudson, Horace B., *A Half Century of Minneapolis*, The Hudson Publishing Company, New York, 1908. Re. Dr. Frederick A. Dunsmoor, Henry F. Brown, p. 35 land titles.

Irvine, J.B., *South Dakota Historical Collections*, Volume X, about 1921, Ref. M.H.S. *F605.1 .B8717 and F 646 .S76. Pg. 362, 371-374, 377, 382 - "A Steam Wagon Invented by an Early Resident of South Dakota [Joseph Renshaw Brown]."

Jones and Brekke, *The Minnesota Almanac*, 1976 and 1981. P. 34, re. "Minisota."

Jones, Robert F., 1928 booklet Eighteenth Annual Edition, *The Story of Longfellow Gardens*. Primary source of Longfellow Gardens material. It tells of "governess carts" at pony ring and wintering of ponies at the zoo.

Kennedy, Roger, *Men on the Moving Frontier*, 1969. Footnote - p. 52 - Joseph R. Brown worked for Indian policies in line with ideals of General Henry Hastings Sibley.

Layton, Robert, *Dvorak Symphonies and Concertos*, British Broadcasting Corporation, 1978.

Longfellow, Henry Wadsworth, *The Song of Hiawatha*, 1855.

Mason, Philip P., Editor, *Schoolcraft's Expedition to Lake Itasca: The Discovery of the Source of the Mississippi*, Michigan State University Press, 1958. This gives accounts of Joseph R. Brown's rather unpleasant encounter with explorer Henry Rowe Schoolcraft on the St. Croix River in 1832, in journals by Lt. Allen, Dr. Houghton and Schoolcraft.

McDermott, John Francis, *Seth Eastman's Mississippi*, University of Illinois Press, 1973.

___, Seth Eastman, *Pictorial Historian of the Indian*, University of Oklahoma Press, 1961.

Meyer, Ellen Wilson, *Happenings Around Excelsior, 1853-1953*, published 1982. Re. Doctor Edward Perkins, one-time miller at Minnetonka City.

Minneapolis Aquatennial Association and Minneapolis Centennial Committee, *Minneapolis, City of Opportunity, A Century of Progress in the Aquatennial City*, T.S. Denison and Company, Minneapolis, 1956. Colonel Snelling, Major Taliaferro, Fort Snelling, Philander Prescott, Chief Cloud Man, Pierre Bottineau helps build Stevens house, pg. 38, Ard Godfrey, Col. John H. Stevens, background material.

Minnesota House of Representatives, *Facts About Minnesota* brochure, 1988, part of a tourism booklet, *Explore Minnesota, Facts and Figures*.

Mitchell, W.H. and J.H. Stevens, *History of the County of Hennepin*, 1868. Pg. 22 and 23 re. land claims on military reservation used in Godfrey chapter.

Montgomery, D.H., *The Leading Facts of American History*, Ginn & Company, The Athenaeum Press, 1902. P. 230 - map showing Michigan and Missouri Territories, 1821.

Morris, H.S., *Historical Stories and Legends of Northeastern South Dakota*, 1889-1939.

Pg. 76 and 77, a short biography of Joseph R. Brown. American Indians called him "Crooked Foot" because of maiming from an ax that slipped.

Morris, Lucy Leavenworth Wilder, *Old Rail Fence Corners*, 1976 Reprint, Minnesota Historical Society. Re. Bayard Shaver, Minnetonka Mills and J.R. Brown Pig's Eye story.

Mowry, H. W., *Guide and Directory of Lake Minnetonka, Minnesota*, Lake Minnetonka Printing House, Excelsior, 1884.

Neill, Rev. Edward D. and Charles S. Bryant, History of the Minnesota Valley, Including the Explorers and Pioneers of Minnesota, 1882. P. 155, William Snelling editor of the Boston Herald.

Neill, Edward D., *History of Minnesota from the Earliest French Explorations to the Present Time*, 1883. Brief mention of Brown and Snelling "Minne-Ha-Ha" trip.

___, *History of Minnesota*, 1878, Third Edition, Revised and Enlarged. Re. 1838 Chan Wakan on Grey Cloud Island where Brown lived.

___, *Fort Snelling*, Major-General Jacob Brown, 1888, Reference *F 612 H 5856 . N3, Minnesota Historical Society.

Neill, Rev. Edw. and J. Fletcher Williams, *History of Hennepin County and the City of Minneapolis*, 1881.

Peary, Emily Ross, *Minnehaha Laughing Water*, 1889 booklet.

Poden, Carolyn (cover artist), *History of Edina* booklet, 1975.

Richards, Bergmann, *Minnetonka Beach: 1855-1955*, Minnetonka Beach Civic Association, 1955. Pp. 16-21, 24, 25 — This includes Snelling duel information.

___, *Early Background of Minnetonka Beach*, Hennepin County Historical Society, 1957. Contains valuable newspaper articles by Stevens and Tuttle re. their Lake Minnetonka, April, 1852 discovery trip. *The Excelsior Weekly,* May 30, 1883. See pp. 44-46.

Russell, A.J., *One of Our First Families and a Few Other Minnesota Essays*, 1925. A vivid account of Prescott's escape attempt and death during 1862-63 war between local government and some of the Dakotas.

Sasse, Fred A., *The Dan Patch Story*, 1957.

Schonberg, *The Lives of the Great Composers*, W.W. Norton& Co., Inc., NewYork, 1970.

Schussler, Otto F., M.D., *Pills*, 1924.
___, *Riverside Reveries*, 1928.

Scott, A.I.A. and Jeffrey Hess, *History and Architecture of Edina, Minnesota*, 1981.

Searles, Robert L., Chairman, *Report of the Lake Minnetonka Task Force*, June, 1983.

Snelling, Henry Hunt, *Memoirs of a Boyhood at Fort Snelling*, privately printed, 1939.

Snelling, William Joseph, *Tales of the North west, 1830*; reprinted 1936 by The University of Minnesota, Minneapolis.

Stevens House, *Ancestry of Colonel John Harrington Stevens and His Wife, Frances Helen Miller By Mary Holman*,F.A.S.G., 1948. Confirms Puritan ancestry.

Stubbs, Roger Avery, *Historic Minnetonka Mills, Gateway to Lake Minnetonka*, 1985, available Minnetonka Library. Jennie Atwood Pratt interview of June 30, 1947 (when she was age one hundred) re. using frogs for dolls, pg. 118, St. John's Episcopal Church, built 1858 — picture, p. 99, and other "Mills" material.

Upham, Warren, *Minnesota Geographic Names*, 1969, Minnesota Historical Society. Re. Brown's Falls name.

West, Ruth and Willis Mason West, *The Story of Our Country*, Allyn and Bacon, Boston, New York, Chicago, 1948.

Wiggins, David S., *Service in "Siberia": Five Surgeons at Early Fort Snelling*, Minnesota Historical Society Press booklet, St. Paul Minnesota, 1977.

Wilson, Blanche Nichols, *Minnetonka Story*, Colwell Press, Inc., Minneapolis, Minnesota, 1950.

Wirth Theodore, *Minneapolis Park System*, 1883-1944, July 16, 1945.

Witteman, A., *Fort Snelling and Minnehaha Falls* booklet, 1898, "Scouting in Minnehaha Creek" picture.